# 110 TALES OF WISDOM

*From All Over the World*

## By the same author

*This book was published in French: Contes de sagesse,* Dangles (2000.

*Sâdhus, Going beyond the dreadlocks,* Prakash Books (New Delhi) 2010
Hindi: Diamond pocket books (New delhi).
Marathi: Padmagandha Prakashan, (Pune).
Tamoul: New Horizons (Chennai).
French: *Sadhus, un voyage initiatique chez les ascètes de l'Inde*, éd. Le Relié, 2009 ; Pocket spiritualité, 2011.

*Le Kabbaliste,* Relié (2002), Pocket Spiritualité 2003.
*Hebrew: HaKabbalist,* éditions Yahel, Tel Aviv, Israël, 2010.

*Dieu croit-il en Dieu ?,* Question de / Albin Michel, 1993.

*Nous sommes tous des idolâtres,* Bayard, 1994.

*Dieu leur parle-t-il ?,* Desclée de Brouwer, 1997 (out of print, available in free loading on the web site of the author).

Contact: levy.patrick@gmail.com
http://site.patricklevy.free.fr/

# 110
# TALES OF WISDOM
## *From All Over the World*

**Patrick Levy**

**Vani**

*A Creative Imprint of Vani Prakashan*

**New Delhi**

www.vaniprakashan.in

First Published in 2012 by Vani Prakashan

21-A, Daryaganj, New Delhi-110002

India.

www.vaniprakashan.in

Vani Prakashan's signature motif is created by Artiste Maqbool Fida Husain.



ISBN: 978-93-5000-965-9

Spirituality/Short Stories



First printing: January 2012, India.

# Foreword

*In his Gospel, John tells of the death of Lazarus: how his sisters grieved, how the crowd gathered from Jerusalem, and then how Jesus arrived four days later and summoned Lazarus from the tomb and resurrected him.*

*According to John, this miracle was to serve Christ who performed it so that "the Son of God may be glorified". No doubt Lazarus must have been happy for he lived a little longer, and his sisters too, for they didn't have to suffer the bereavement. But in what way is this story useful for the reader? How does the reader grow through reading it? Does it teach us to accept the inevitable? Does it help us develop on the path of wisdom?*

*The resurrection of a man is an extremely rare phenomenon in human history. All other living beings die once and for all. Even Lazarus died again sometime afterwards.*
*A woman rushed to the Buddha carrying her dead child*

*in her arms. The Awakened One did not bring the child back to life. "Go to the village and bring back a handful of rice from a house where no one has ever died" he told her. Of course she could not find such a house. Yet her failure meant that she, and ourselves as readers, could develop some lucidity and a little wisdom: life is impermanent; death inevitably curtails it everyone is bound to lose a loved one through death.*

*A wisdom tale differs from a fairytale, a fable or a myth. Even if it is founded on incredible, imaginary or exaggerated circumstances, it never ends with a miracle, nor does it find its resolution in magic or supernatural powers, for such tricks call for faith not wisdom. Wisdom is manifested in unexpected perspectives and responses which inspire the soul, heart and intellect - all at once. What it reveals to us might at times make us say, like the disciples of Rabbi*[1] *Simeon: "If we had only come to this world to hear these words, it would have sufficed us."*

*A wisdom tale does not necessarily attempt to portray moral virtue or ethical conduct. It may, on the contrary, appear immoral, iconoclastic or blasphemous. What is sought is an enlightening effect produced by the sage's clear-sightedness, the boldness of his response, the strength of the truth he is demonstrating,*

[1] A Rabbi is a Jewish priest.

*or simply by the serenity emanating from the solution he suggests.*

*Lastly we should distinguish a wise-man or sage from a saint. A saint is a person that lives his faith thoroughly and completely. He may be a kind hearted man overwhelmed by the suffering of his fellow beings, who somehow shares it to make it lighter; or he himself he ties to share their him and make in lighter suffers to please God, or to redeem the world of its sins... However a sage does not suffer. His compassion doesn't manifest in even more pain and powerlessness, it is expressed in ways that show how to relieve or overcome them.*

*The tradition of wisdom tales stretches back as far as memory itself. It is probably as old as speech and as far reaching as humanity is on earth. Some stories have traveled several times around the world. They are told from Asia to Latin America, in the Middle East and in Central Europe with characters that vary according to ethnical and local colorations and differences. Each storyteller adds to them their own cultural imprints and sensitivities.*

*Using tales, stories, legends and fables chosen from different spiritual horizons, from the biographies of sages (at times slightly modified, as has always been the case) and from accounts inspired by observations and experience, in this book we will try to invoke, without any certainty of having grasped it, this somewhat rare human quality of wisdom.*

# I

## Who is a Sage?

*What is wisdom? Actually, nobody really knows. 'Wisdom is not a thing; it is a whole array of better-than-ordinary ways of being, living, and dealing with the world'. But what is it that makes the difference between better and ordinary? Wisdom is the 'ability to judge correctly and to follow the best course of action, based on knowledge and understanding'. How does knowledge and understanding make us wise? 'It is beyond simply knowing or understanding.' According to Job, 'Wisdom is made up of nothingness'.*[2]

*The wise-man does not preach a doctrine and wisdom does not seem to follow a particular path. Yet a few signs point towards its existence: non-conformism, courage, a bold sense of freedom, inventiveness, an unshakable serenity, enthusiasm, lucidity, candor, a logic carried to its extreme consequences, limitless confidence, a disarming simplicity, a manner of awareness, and sometimes even a little madness...*

---

[2]. Job 28: 20;

## The crops which will bring madness

'I have read in the stars that the next harvest will bring madness to everyone who eats it,' told a king to his counselor. 'What do you suggest we do?'
'The problem is not insoluble, your Majesty,' replied the counselor. 'We will not eat of it. We will commandeer what remains of last year's harvest and will eat it, you and me, next year.'
'What about the others?'
'Your Majesty, there are not enough reserves to feed everyone. But there will be enough for you and me.'
'Impossible!' the king exclaimed. 'How can we remain sane while our subjects are struck with madness? That means we would be estranged from our very own people! No, we shall participate and share in this madness, for if we remain sane in an insane world the mad people will think we are mad anyway.
But we shall keep the memory of this decision. We will etch our foreheads with the sign of madness. Thus, whenever I look at you, and whenever you look at me, we shall both know that we are mad.'[3]

*The sign of madness is, of course, this very story itself. The wisdom here reminds us that the world may be seen as mad. The wise read the signs and etch new ones to avoid getting lost.*

---

[3]. Rabbi Nahman of Bratzlav, *The Tales*, Arnold J. Baud, Paulist Press, 1988.

# Recognizing wisdom

An old sadhu lived as a hermit on the top of a hill, far from the concerns of the world.

One day, he received a visit by a man from a neighbouring village.

'It has not rained for two years and the crops have been scarce; the last crop will be completely lost,' he explained. 'Dearth will soon become famine as we are now drawing on the grain reserved for sowing just to eat. And then, what will we have to sow when the rain returns next year?'

The man explained this situation to the sage and asked for his advice.

The sage said:

'Each villager must bring together all the grain they have. Eat half of it to survive and sow the other half, but only in the most fertile plots. You must cultivate them together. Water them with water from the wells. And when the harvest is ready you will share it together. Now the rich are as poor as the poor. This is an opportunity to change and to learn to share.'

'You are a wise man!' the villager exclaimed.

Bowing to him, the sadhu replied humbly:

'No, the wise man is the one who can recognize wisdom.'

*So, dear reader, when you find some wisdom in these stories, you'll know you are already wise.*

## The philosopher

A young man once sought out a philosopher and questioned him:
'I want to be wise. How can I achieve my goal?'
The philosopher sighed and said, whilst staring at the walls of his office, covered with shelves of books up to the ceiling:
'One of these books tells the story of a young man who went to an old philosopher to get some directions on the path to wisdom. The old philosopher uttered a deep sigh and said: "Long ago, a young man who looked very much like you, wanted to be wise. His desire was very strong. One day he found himself face to face with a philosopher, just like us right now, and he asked him: How can I become wise?"
One often takes the philosophers who have studied philosophy to be philosophers who have found wisdom and loved it,' the first philosopher concluded.[4]

*Perhaps there are no wise men but only apprentices on the path of wisdom. Perhaps the beginning of wisdom is knowing that you will always never be anything more than an apprentice.*

[4]. Liberally adapted from a Sufi tale.

# Finding your way

*'Who would be foolish enough to die without having, at least once, made the rounds of his prison?'*

*–Marguerite Yourcenar.*

When he was a teenager, Louis was an average student. He had never really made any effort to pretend that he believed in what he was told to learn and repeat.

Later, he had difficulties adjusting to his first jobs. He was asked to perform repetitive tasks for which he could find no interest. The submissiveness required in the working environment was an unbearable burden for him. He was bored, and worse, he was wasting his life away.

His parents expected him to get married, start a family, and raise children. They hoped he would settle down, be successful, buy an apartment and a nice car, open a savings account, and provide for his retirement. But this lifestyle had no appeal for him at all. He refused to be subjected to conformity, to living in fear and he resisted the temptation of having his life hemmed into a narrow path in the name of security. He preferred to stay light, free from constraints and worries. In short, he wanted life to be a gift, a playful adventure, rather than a sum of duties and responsibilities. And he was ready to affront the risks this involved.

One day he resigned from his job, gave leave of his flat and left to travel the world.

'When will you come back?' his parents asked him.

'Each time you leave your home you take your key with you,

so you've already decided you'll return. If you travel with a return ticket, you don't really leave, you go on a journey. I have no key and no return ticket," he replied.
He bid farewell saying: 'Tagore said "Where roads are made, I lose my way." I'm going to follow Tagore in different ways.'[5]

[5]. This last line is by Rabindranath Tagore, *Gitanjali, 1912.*

# What is Truth?

A man wanted to find out the absolute and definitive Truth. First he methodically dedicated himself to all kinds of pleasures the world has to offer. He pursued the delights of sensual pleasures, explored the alchemy of scents, colours, sounds and flavours. He investigated the subtleties of taste and the refined gracefulness of style and voluptuousness. He learned to appreciate the most delicious wines and the finest foods and how to give and receive the most exquisite caress. But soon the pleasures faded and he became bored of them. There was no absolute truth in them. Where was the Truth to be found?

He began to travel around the globe to meet with all kinds of priests, shamans, medicine men, sorcerers, magicians, astrologers, witch-doctors, soothsayers, sages and miracle workers that the world has produced. Yet he could only ever find fragments of truth in their knowledge. He was never completely satisfied in his search for absolute Truth. He returned home a little disappointed, yet he felt enriched by a new discovery: *there is no absolute Truth to be found elsewhere or in anyone.* Even though he hadn't found Truth, he continued to search for it. Now remaining in his home, without venturing out any further, he studied all the religions, practiced all kinds of asceticism, prayed, praised, worshipped and exhorted all the gods that have ever been prayed to, praised, worshiped or exhorted since the beginning of time. One day he stopped all such practices. He was a little disappointed, but was once again enriched with a new discovery: *there is no evidence*

*about any God or anything beyond the here and now.* He even saw one can have no certainty about that either.
He was now an old man.
However he still wondered what was the Truth? Then, on his sixtieth birthday he realized he had always wrong. He thought he had been seeking Truth, but in fact, all along he had only been trying to find certainties. He now knew that certainty cannot be found anywhere.
When the man was finally on the threshold of death, (and still ignorant of what this might bring), he finally found some truth: *uncertainty is the fundamental fact of life, and also its driving force and a space within which freedom can be found; it is the very root of spirituality, and a source of real joy.*

# Bodhidharma

Bodhidharma, the youngest son of the king of Ceylon, was born around 500 AD. His tutor was the great master Hannya Tara.

One day, the king gave Hannya Tara a jewel of priceless value. Bodhidharma's tutor asked him and his two brothers:

'Is there in the whole world a single thing more valuable than this stone?'

The elder prince responded with praise:

'Our master is in possession of the most beautiful treasure in the world!'

The second prince said:

'Even if we were to search the world over for our whole life, we wouldn't find such a jewel.'

In turn Bodhidharma, who was only eight years old, said:

'This stone is a great treasure, a valuable treasure, but it's a treasure of this world. Understanding its value is a form of wisdom, but it is not profound wisdom. The true wisdom, which is more valuable than the greatest treasure, is to understand ourselves, because in understanding oneself one understands all men.'[6]

*The Ancient Greeks also taught us: 'Know yourself and you shall know the universe and its Gods,'* and Thomas said: *'Whoever finds himself, the world is not worthy of him.'*[7]

---

[6]. From *History of Buddhism*, Keisai, 1976, Tokyo.

[7]. The Gospels of Thomas, Logia 111.

# Solomon

*Solomon isn't known for praying to God for power or glory... He is celebrated for his wisdom. Let us look at the story of the decision that earned this sage his fame.*

Two prostitutes came to King Solomon and stood before him. One of them said:

'My lord, this woman and I live in the same house; and I gave birth to a baby while she was in the house with me. Then on the third day after I gave birth, this woman also gave birth. And we were alone. There was no one else; there were only the two of us in the house. This woman's son died in the night, because she was lying on him. So she got up in the middle of the night and took my son from my side while I, your servant, was sleeping. She took him to her breast and laid her dead son at my breast. When I rose in the morning to feed my child, behold he was dead. But when I looked at him more closely, behold, he was not the child that I had borne.'

The second woman interrupted, 'No, the child that is alive is mine, and the dead child is yours.' Then the first one retorted, 'No, the dead child is yours, and the living child is mine.' Thus they argued before the king.

Then the king said, 'One says, "This is my son that is alive, and your son is dead"; and the other says, "No; your son is dead, and mine is alive."'

The king then requested, 'Bring me a sword.' So a sword was brought before the king.

So the king said, 'Divide the living child in two; half shall be given to one and half to the other.'

The second woman said, 'This way he shall neither be mine nor yours; divide him in two.'

'Oh, my lord, give her the living child, but by no means put him to death,' exclaimed the first woman.

Then the king answered and said, 'Give the living child to the first woman, and by no means put him to death; she is his mother.'

It is said that all Israel heard of the judgment the king had rendered, and they stood in awe of him, because in his justice they perceived the wisdom of God.

'If we look carefully, in fact, we don't know for sure if the woman who was willing to give up the living child was actually his mother,' commented Rabbi Isaac Goldman before his disciples gathered around the long study table. 'What we do know is that to keep the child alive, one of the two women agreed to give him to the other.

Under what law and the application of which principle, did Solomon render his judgment? There are no such laws and principles. To satisfy both plaintiffs, Solomon decided to cut the child in two. Even though he did not know who the mother of the child was, he did something to find out which of the two women was a mother.

Solomon sought what was right and just rather than true, and what was just probably revealed the truth. His wisdom was his ability to let go of truth. He made a judgment, then had no hesitation in cancelling it. He therefore rendered two judgments for a single concern. Rather than avoiding the problem, he dealt with it. He did not enforce a law, a tradition or a regulation; he found a solution. That is what wisdom is."[8]

8. I King 2 16-28.

## Two Karmapas for one Throne
(A tale of anticipation)

Tibet had already been occupied by China for a long time when His Holiness the sixteenth Karmapa, the head of the Karma Kagyu lineage, died in exile.

The four regents of the lineage were taking care of routine affairs while seeking the new birth of their great master. But the years passed. The Chinese occupation of Tibet hadn't helped things.

One day, Tai Situ Rinpoche, one of the four regents, remembered a precious reliquary that the Karmapa had given him. He examined it carefully and inside he found a letter from His Holiness Karmapa giving specific indications concerning his future birth place. It would be in Tibet, in the province of Kham. So Tai Situ sent a delegation of monks to look for him and eventually they found a child, Urgyen Trinley Dorje, who matched the information left by the late Karmapa.

However Shamar Rinpoche, also a regent, accused Tai Situ Rinpoche of having forged a fake document, and he claimed to have discovered the new birth of the Karmapa: Trinley Thaye Dorje, the son of Mipham Rinpoche.

So there were two tulkus. Both successfully passed the traditional authentication tests. Both were enthroned, but by different religious and political organizations. The Dalai Lama recognized Urgyen Trinley Dorje as the tulku of the sixteenth Karmapa. But Shamar Rinpoche persisted in his conviction of having found the true rebirth of the master and enthroned Trinley Thaye Dorje.

The Tibetan community in exile was divided. In New Delhi, Gangtok and Rumtek, supporters and followers of both regents even came to blows! Some were wounded and a few even died. After this the regents couldn't go anywhere without bodyguards!

Things soured further when Shamar Rinpoche accused Tai Situ Rinpoche of being a spy for China and informed the Indian government. Since Sino-Indian relations were already strained, Tai Situ was banned from India, the place of his own monastery, for ten years.

As for Tai Situ, he found an old text, written by Guru Rinpoche, in which the founder of Tibetan Buddhism had prophesied that between the sixteenth and seventeenth rebirth of the Karmapa, a regent would sow discord. He strongly suggested that this regent was none other than Shamar Rinpoche. But the argument was unconvincing to the supporters of Shamar Rimpoche, because Guru Rinpoche lived in the eighth century and at this time the Karmapa lineage had not yet come into existence. It had started in the twelfth century.

Buddhist devotees and friends all over the world were forced to choose sides!

What was all this about?

Years passed with new disclosures and new attacks. Some tried to calm things down arguing that the two regents had secretly worked together to organize this chaos and actually protect the real Karmapa from the Chinese government, who they suspected of wanting to kidnap him. Others suggested that the wisdom of the Karmapa was putting the Buddhist community to the test. Many expected that the fake Karmapa

would die on the day of his great enthronement.
Both tulkus grew up to become worthy representatives of the Karma Kagyu tradition, both were scholars and sages. Both were praiseworthy Bodhisattvas, Emanations of Buddhahood. One day, they were both invited to an official meeting, but each one had no idea that the other was also expected to attend. Both tulkus came face to face for the first time. Contrary to all expectations, they bowed deeply to one another.
The first said:
'O Supreme Conqueror of the cycle of births, I prostrate to you and I step aside to the perfectly self enlightened one.'
'I see that since beginningless time you have repeatedly been my own mother' the other replied. I'm the one who should step aside, O Emanation of Right action. You are the Seventeenth Karmapa.'
'Sangye, you eliminate obstructions and illuminate with knowledge. I have no memory of being Karmapa while you are undoubtedly the Healer of all evils, the perfectly clear mind, the Supreme Bliss Body, the Seventeenth Karmapa.
'The cycle of births and liberation are one and the same phenomenon. O Light of the World, Illuminator of the Knowledge of True Wisdom, my mind has no notion of a previous life.'
The audience was stunned by this unexpected exchange of bowing and civility. With each reply supporters of each side saw their hopes of victory vanish a little more, but they also slowly understood the insignificance of their disputes.
'Birth and Rebirth, existence and nonexistence, obscured mind and the pure nature of the mind, O Destroyer of the pride of

all disputers, Perfectly Radiant One, nothing alters in you the unified vision of unaltered un-obscured mind. Please guide us all on the path of wisdom.

'O Treasury of perfect excellence, the nature of rebirth is very subtle. We cannot prove the existence of a previous life, yet it cannot be established either that there isn't one. Rebirth is a theory and any conceptual certainty forms an obscuration on the formless mind. Disputes are vain and without foundation. No self, no determination of a self. O Tathagata, Sure One, Supreme Emanation Body of Emptiness, I beg you to head the lineage. Fountain of Nectar that quenches the thirst for knowledge; please accept the Karmapa's throne.

'The mind is the essence of all things. The mind has every possibility, one Karmapa, two Karmapas, or even no Karmapa at all. O perfectly clear mind, Embodiment of the nature of the mind, Teacher of the gods and of humans, take the throne of Karmapa and may your Holiness accept me as a faithful disciple.'

'Was there a Karmapa? Is there a Karmapa? Which one of us is Karmapa? All beings are Karmapas! Omnipotent founder of the lineage, you dispel the darkness of ignorance. Liberated and Liberator of all, world honoured Enlightened One, I request you to be my guru.'

'Limitless Mind, free of obstacles, unborn, uncreated, Heir to the Supreme Knowledge, free from birth and death, Master of Dharma, Lord of the World, I have nothing to teach you. Take the throne, fulfil the wishes of all beings, and dry up the great ocean of suffering.'

'Form is empty and emptiness is form. O Quintessence of the

enlightened mind, not even conceiving of emptiness, surpassing any conceptions, Self-existent, Illuminator of the Great Torch, we all beg you to accept the throne out of compassion for the sangha (community).'

Hours passed this way. They offered each other the role of Supreme Rinpoche tirelessly. It became increasingly obvious that neither of them wanted to have it and that they'd rather abstain. At the end of this meeting, there would probably be no Karmapa left.

'No desire, no need. Only the wish to retire to a hermitage and practice for the benefit of all beings. Emanation of all the Buddhas' activities, absolute Ruler over all law, Embodiment of Buddha as Karmapa, you are the Victorious One, the inspiration of all sentient beings.'

'O Precious Omniscient, accomplished Master who makes the ignorant wise, you will teach innumerable beings as they become fit to be taught; you will attract all beings by your knowledge.'

'O Light of the World, Illuminator of the Knowledge of True Wisdom, set the Wheel of Law in motion again for the benefit of all beings.'

At that time, Tai Situ Rinpoche interceded.

'As a Regent of the lineage of the Karma Kagyu, I say that both are indisputably Karmapa! Both Karmapas will head the Karma Kagyu lineage.'

Shamar Rinpoche then said:

'Buddha's infinite compassion is manifested in two Karmapas. Whatever the circumstances of their birth, they have become learned in all learning, fully realized, having obtained the ultimate knowledge. Accept your destiny and both become heads of the Karma Kagyu school.

The two tulkus embraced, gently joining their foreheads in mutual respect.[9]

[9]. A fictional tale based on fact.

## Yudhishtira the wise

*Yudhishtira is one of the heroes from the Mahabharata, the Hindu epic that tells the story of Gods and men from the very beginning. He was the son of Yama, the first man, lord of virtue and ruler of the kingdom of death. Calm, balanced in his judgments, incorruptible, Yudhishtira is considered to be the fairest and the wisest of men.*
*One day, Dharma, the father of mankind, appeared before him in the guise of an elf and questioned him:*

'What is swifter than the Wind?'
'Mind is swifter than the wind'
'What is more prolific than grass?'
'There are more thoughts arising in the mind of a man than grass in the fields.'
'What is true asceticism?'
'Controlling the mind.'
'What is the highest refuge of virtue?'
'Generosity.'
'What is the safest protection from fame?'
'Kindness is the safest protection from fame.'
'What is the safest shelter for thoughts?'
'Truth.'
'And for happiness, what is the safe haven?'
'Patience.'
'What is patience?'
'Taming senses and desires leads to patience.'
'Of all the shelters, which is the highest?'

'Giving.'
'What, if renounced, makes one kind and agreeable?'
'Pride, if renounced, makes one become kind and agreeable.'
'What is pride?'
'Pride is believing you are the one who plays out your life.'
'What is the essential nature of forgiveness?'
'Forgiveness consists in enduring hostility.'
'How can one avoid the shame?'
'By renouncing unworthy acts.'
'Tell me what enemy is invisible?'
'Anger.'
'What disease is most difficult to treat?'
'Greed.'
'What is the cause of sorrow?'
'Immoderate attachment.'
'What is the breeding ground of suffering?'
'Impatience.'
'What is wickedness?'
'Seeing evil rather than good.'
'What is compassion?'
'Wishing happiness for all beings.'
'What is charity?'
'Protecting all creatures.'
'Which man can be considered dishonest?'
'He who has no pity is dishonest.'
'Who is the most fortunate man?'
'The most fortunate man has risen above pleasure and frustration, happiness and sorrow, past and future.'
'What is the best of all kinds of happiness?'

'Contentment.'

'What is the best of all qualities worthy of being praised?'

'Skill.'

'What is laziness?'

'Not performing one's duties is laziness.'

'What is duty?'

'Doing what you have to do to your best ability without expecting a particular outcome, an impervious outlook that is equal in success and in failure. In action, it is acting without attachment to the object or the act, leaving things in their virgin state and their anonymity.'

'What is the highest of all duties?'

'To abstain from harming anyone is the first of all duties.'

'What, if you renounce it, brings you no regrets?'

'If hope is renounced, one doesn't regret it.'

'What is tranquillity?'

'Control over emotions.'

'How does one control emotions?'

'By abstaining from judging, remaining steadfast in the vision of unity within duality. Then, pleasure and displeasure, hot and cold, pride and humility are the two sides of the same coin.'

'What is simplicity?'

'Equanimity is perfectly simple. It is seeing gold, earth and stone in the same light. It is to look upon a saint, a dog and someone who eats dogs in the same way.'

'What is the most precious kind of renouncement?'

'The renunciation of desire, because desire is that which accords preciousness to things.'

'What is the essential nature of desire?'

'Desires originate in ideas, and ideas are born in the mind. When the mind is controlled, the senses are controlled. One can resolutely remain in oneself.'

'What is true cleanliness?'

'When taking a bath, it is also washing the mind clean of all impurities.'

'What is the cause of suffering?'

'Illusion'

'What is illusion?'

'Forms and desires weave appearances. Knowledge of the real is beyond these.'

'What is real in this world?'

'Neither this nor that. Beyond space and time. Beyond form. Only the formless is everlasting.'

'What, if we neglect it, leads to error?'

'Forgetting that everything is one being only.'

'What is the most valuable possession?'

'Knowledge.'

'What is true knowledge?'

'Awareness that has awareness as an object.'

'What gives rise to knowledge?'

'Stillness. Awareness is the sacrifice and awareness is the offering. Awareness is the one to whom all this happens. The fire of knowledge reduces everything to ashes. Immortality is found in the remnants of sacrifice.'

'In action what remains motionless?'

'Action in the body, non-action in the mind.'

'What is the best religion?'

'The best religion leads men to free themselves from fear.'
'What is the Way?'
'Those who are good show the Way.'
'What is the right Way?'
'The sacred texts all differ from each other. There is not even one rishi whose opinion can be accepted as infallible. Concerning religion and duty, truth is hidden in solitude and silence. This is the place where, along with the Greats, we can meditate on the Way.'[10]

[10]. Adapted from Mahabharata, Yaksha-prasna, with added verses from the Bhagavad Gîtâ.

# Be yourself

There was once a man who wanted to be like Rama, an avatar of Vishnu who was King of Ayodya, or like Krishna who is the great teacher of the Bhagawata gita... He dreamt of becoming a scholar that even the Gods would listen to, like Shankaracharya. He would have loved to be a poet - the new Tagore, or a philosopher like Vivekananda, or someone who could create and sing songs of praise to the Gods like Kabir... However, he had nothing extraordinary to say, and no one listened to him.

He decided he would become a saint. He studied the scriptures and the sacred laws, practiced devotion and prayed... At least, he did this according to his not so great abilities. Praying bored him; he did not understand much about the Sanskrit treaties, and although he did good around him, he was far from being noticed as a benefactor of humanity.

When he realized that, all things considered, saintliness was not watching out for him, that he would never be an avatar or a saint, he decided to become very rich so that he could be immensely generous. But his outlandish plans to make his own fortune almost brought about his ruin. He lamented at length that he would never be a great man, neither in this world nor the after world.

One day, he met swami Anandababa.

'When I move on to the after world, I won't be asked: "Why were you not Sankaracharia or Tagore?" I shall be asked: "Why were you not Anandababa?"' swami Anandababa told him.[11]

[11]. Adapted from *Hassidism : The Movement and its Masters ; Jason Aronson Inc. ;* 1988. And from Martin Buber, Tales of the Hasidim.

# Breaking the mountain

*Some of us wish they were someone else, different... if I had, if I were, if only, one day when I... I'll be satisfied, happy, fulfilled.*

Once upon a time, there was a poor man whose job was to break rocks from the mountain, turning them into gravel that would be used to build roads. He toiled every day long hours under the hot sun, pounding and banging those boulders. One day the king of the land came to pass by near where the poor man was working. He was riding a beautiful horse and was wearing all the finery of his royal position. While he was pounding and banging, the poor man thought:

'Oh, if I were king, what power I would have! I would ride through my kingdom and bestow many good deeds upon my subjects...'

The Great Almighty of Heaven heard his thoughts and made him a king. Now as a king, he travelled his kingdom on horseback, dressed in the rich and heavy clothing befitting his status, and he bestowed his grace and generosity upon his subjects. But the sun was scorching and the king was suffocating. 'Ah! If I were the sun, what power I would have!' thought the king. 'I would bring people light and be the source of great blessings...'

The Great Almighty of Heaven heard his thoughts and transformed the king into a sun. Now as a sun, he brought light to everyone from dawn to dusk and radiated his beneficent warmth. But a cloud passed by in the sky and hid the sun, and

a shadow covered the face of the earth.
'Oh, no! The sun is not so mighty after all,' said the sun. 'If I were a cloud, what power I would have! I would choose rain or shine, and I would be a source of great blessings for people...'
And the Great Almighty of Heaven heard these words and transformed the sun into a large and heavy cloud. He would make rain at the right time and farmers would have lavish harvests. But one day, he realized he could not go beyond the mountain, for it was too high.
'Oh,' lamented the cloud, 'clouds are not so powerful after all. The mountains are mightier', he thought. 'If I were a mountain, I would be a welcome shade for people and I would protect and shield them from forceful winds...'
Hearing these words, the Great Almighty of Heaven transformed him into a mountain. And the mountain was very proud. But looking at his feet, what did he see? A poor old man who was breaking parts of his rocks into gravel that would be used to make roads...[12]

[12]. Adapted from a tale from ancient China.

# Non-dependency

Obaku was a disciple of Master Nansen and followed his teaching for several years even though he had never obtained a private audience with him. One day master Nansen finally granted him an interview and asked him:
'What does it mean to attain enlightenment or see Buddha nature?'
'I don't want to depend on anything,' said Obaku. 'I do not wish to obtain enlightenment either through intelligence or wisdom. So I don't even depend on non-dependence. If I attach importance to the Buddha, I remain below Buddha. So I have to jump on the Buddha's head to move forward.'
The master answered:
'A blue sky and a bright day. Needless to seek Buddha around us.'

*The ultimate desire is to have no desire! Contentment is being aware of what is.*[13]

[13]. *Two Zen Classics : Mumonkan and Hekiganroku*, Weatherhill, 1977. Thirtieth cases.

## Save yourself and Save the world

A sadhu was living in a street in Varanasi. It was the cold season, and nights were biting and chilly, so the sadhu had gathered a supply of used plastic shopping bags and he was slowly burning them to warm himself up.

I was with three friends, Vishnu, Prakash and Ganesh. We sat with him. Vishnu explained in his scientific way that burning plastic bags produces dioxin fumes, which everyone breathes in the air, and that dioxin fumes can produce cancer in the lungs, weaken the central nervous system and the immune system.

'Agni is fire. Agni is the ultimate end of everything,' the sadhu answered. 'Agni purifies everything!'

'Actually, in this case, Agni does not,' Vishnu told him. 'You may not see it anymore, but the smoke produced by your fire it is still there, in the air; it is just invisible. So fire is not the proper way to dispose of plastic bags because it doesn't destroy them, it just transforms them into toxic fumes.'

'Atchaaa!' the saint exclaimed.

But Prakash saw that he was not yet convinced. So employing the sadhu's mythology, he told him: 'The fumes of the plastic bags are like Asuras (demons); we don't see them, but they act inside your body.' And in yet another way: 'You must offer Agni only pure materials, like wood or cow dung. Plastic is not a pure material because it's not produced by nature,' he maintained, attempting to educate his devotion. 'If you breathe the smoke from your bonfire of plastic bags, your body will become impure,' he insisted, now bringing purity into issues of the body, where I personally don't believe it belongs. 'And we will all be sick,' he pressed even further now including worries and guilt in his cocktail of arguments. Dried cow dung cakes are cheap. So Ganesh gave a shop keeper enough money to supply the sadhu with four dung cakes a day for a long period. 'It's a drop in the ocean, but that's how we save ourselves and the world,' he told us with humility.

# II

## Masters and Disciples

*Can wisdom be taught? Who can teach it? Can it be acquired through listening to a wise man? By being guided by one? Or by imitating one?*

*History has handed down to us various tales of wisdom, yet in the news we often hear stories of false gurus and their abuse of authority. So what are the real gurus like?*

*A guru or a master has a perfect command of a particular area of expertise. There are math gurus, dance or music gurus... In spiritual traditions, the guru is an 'awakener': 'He dispels darkness and ignorance by revealing a foundational point of view on reality.' He does not attempt to make the disciple use his consciousness as a substitute for their own; his role is to awaken the disciple's consciousness.*

*A spiritual master can be recognised by the coherence between his doctrine, his speech and his actions. Furthermore, the master gives his teaching out of his love of wisdom, compassion for humanity, or simply without any particular goal. He gives what he has to offer, and expects nothing in return. Finally, what he teaches makes the disciple progress, so that he may also in turn become a master, a master of himself. The purpose of their relationship is the attainment of full independence and freedom with regards to each other and with regards to circumstances. But of course, sometimes unexpected detours sneak in between an ideal and its accomplishment.*

## Master, who was your master?

Hasan, the great Sufi master, was dying. One of his disciples asked him:

'Master, who was your master?'

Hasan replied:

'I had thousands of masters. Simply naming them would take months, perhaps years. But I'll tell you about three of them:

The first was a thief.

One day, I was lost in a desert, and when at last I reached a village, it was very late and everything was closed. Finally, I came across a man who was trying to bore a hole in the wall of a house. I asked him if there was a place I could spend the night. He replied saying it would be difficult to find somewhere at that time of night.

"But you can come to my place", he said, "if you don't mind staying with a thief."

I lived with him for a whole month. Every night, he would go out to work. When he left he would say: "Pray and meditate!"

When he returned I would ask:

"Have you found anything?"

"No, nothing tonight. But tomorrow I'll try again, and God willing..."

He was never downcast; he was always happy, joyful and full of faith.

Since then, I have spent years and years in meditation and nothing has ever happened, no visitation from God nor any kind of extraordinary phenomenon. Often, when I was most desperate, when I felt like giving up, I remembered the thief who told me every night: "God willing, maybe tomorrow it will happen".

My second guru was a dog.

I was thirsty one day and I came to a river when a dog arrived there too. He also was thirsty. He bent down towards the water and saw a dog peering back. It was his own reflection. But he was fearful; he barked and ran away, yet he was so thirsty that he kept having to return. Finally in spite of his fear he jumped into the river. So the other dog disappeared. As for me, I saw in this a sign from God: even though you may be afraid, you have to jump.

The third teacher was a child.

I was walking through a small town when I saw a boy holding a lighted candle. He was taking it to the mosque. Jokingly, I asked him:

"Did you light this candle yourself?"

"Yes sir," he replied.

I asked again:

"Before, the candle was not lit, then after the candle was lit. So where did the light come from?"

Then the boy laughed, blew out the candle and said:

"And now you've seen the light go away. Where has it gone? Can you tell me?"

I was shaken. At that moment I saw how stupid I was, how all the knowledge I believed myself to possess as a Scholar, was in fact uncertain. I have never played the great learned man since.

I have not had a single master, but I was a disciple' Hasan concluded. 'Life was my teacher because I learned something from everything it brought to me.'[14]

---

[14]. Rûmi : *In the Arms of the Beloved*, translation by Jonathan Star, The Putnam Publishing Group, 1997. Lee Llewellyn Vaughan, *Travelling the Path of Love*, The golden Sufi centre, 1994. Also told by Bhagwan Shree Rajneesh.

## The first companion

*A wise man chooses to tell the truth rather than words of appeasement. Even if it is brutal, only the truth can really guide us and help us build our life. Progress comes through being clear with each other rather than sharing of illusions or beliefs. Truth is a real master.*

Abbot Pierre tells of how the very first of his Emmaus companions was the survivor of an attempted suicide. This man had killed his father in a fit of desperate rage. He had been reprieved after twenty years in prison, yet feeling hopeless and unemployed, he had tried to kill himself.
Abbot Pierre was called for help and he tried to speak to the man, but he would not listen: his only desire was to attempt and this time succeed in committing suicide.
'Then,' said the abbot, 'I did not do the charitable thing, but I did the opposite. Rather than saying, 'I'll give you a home, a job, money because you are unhappy,' I chose to tell him the truth: 'You are terribly unhappy and I have nothing to give you. I have no money. The house needs doing up and everyone who comes in need and sorrow has to be greeted. I'm torn between my work, greeting newcomers and doing up the hostel, I can't carry out so many duties. I'm weary. But since you want to die and you have nothing that burdens you, give me your life, give me your life by helping me, so that in turn we can help others'.
He agreed.
The man was not just lacking the means to live, but more

particularly the reasons to live. This is how the Emmaus community was born. The companions have nothing to give except their friendship, and their efforts to assist others, together.[15]

[15]. From a radio interview with Abbot Pierre.

# Destiny is how we play Fate

When he was a child, John didn't want to be the son of his parents. He considered them much too ordinary. He liked to fantasize that he was the abandoned child of a prince, an oil tycoon or a wealthy lady who would one day come and free him from mediocrity. For a long time he had no idea that half of the other children have similar fantasies.

Later, as a teenager, he was not a happy person. He found himself to be neither handsome nor interesting, and he despised himself so much that he didn't take time to develop his own qualities. He was unable to see the beauty of the world and discover the treasures to be found in culture.

He sought love but found only selfish pleasures. His lack of self respect meant he was unable to respect, understand or appreciate others. So others rejected him, leaving him isolated in the bitter solitude of his own insensitivity.

As a young man, John rebelled against life and the world. His self-hatred was projected onto everything he judged and he judged just about everything. 'Society' was the object he most liked to blame. In turn he became a Maoist, an anarchist, a Punk and then a fascist. He even spent some time in a sect whose doctrine focused on the sins of mankind, its wickedness, flaws, and weaknesses. Its founding messiah preached a rigorous and exclusive moral order.

One day, one of his friends, who was more curious about life than he was, suggested attending a conference that Anila Rinchen, a woman Lama visiting the city, would give that evening. John agreed to go along yet he fostered an ulterior motive to make trouble.

However that evening some of the Anila's words caught his attention and he listened:

'No human being wants to cause harm. Whatever someone does, it's not their primary goal. The cause of evil is not evil, but fear, and in particular the fear of pain. We do what we do and we are the way we are because we can neither be better nor worse than the way we are. And we should try to accept others as they are as well, because they too can be no different, better or worse than they are.

First, we must learn to understand how a human being operates rather than how he or she should act according to this or that moral code, dogma, or ideal. This is done by examining ourselves. If we observe our actions, our words and our mind, we observe the actions, words and mind of all beings. And then we understand what creates suffering and what creates happiness, for ourselves and everyone else.'

At the end of the conference, the *Anila* held private interviews with anyone who wished to talk to her. John asked for an interview. He sat opposite the nun and assumed his usual posture of hostility. The Anila met his gaze, yet there was no power struggle. There was a complete absence of confrontation in her eyes which gradually dissolved the young man's hatred. He momentarily experienced a feeling of melting into the nun's gaze which was like an ocean of compassion and understanding. She took his hand in a sisterly gesture, and without knowing all the details it was as if she understood all the suffering that had accumulated in him for so many years: his imprisonment in a destructive mentality, his negative emotions and his unspoken, but instinctive desire to free himself from them.

John had just experienced, for the first time, a few moments of unconditional love. The *Anila* said:

'Hope leads to fear, and fear renews hope. When we are held captive by these two tensions, we get caught in the cycle of circumstances consisting of the three poisons of life: desire which can develop into greed and lust; hatred which includes jealousy, anger and aversion; and ignorance or delusion.

Give up hoping to be someone else. Accept who and what you are, because we only start living our life when we accept it as it is.

Fate is the hand of cards life deals us: our parents, the country we are born in, its climate, our genetic and cultural heritage, and why not, even our astrological horoscope as well! Destiny is the way we play that hand of fate. We cannot change fate, but we can change the way we play', Anila Rinchen explained.

'I'm not asking you to love everyone; just try not to add suffering to suffering. This will be the beginning of your own deliverance from suffering.'

*The Dalai Lama teaches 'Sow an act, and you reap a habit; sow a habit, and you reap a character; sow a character, and you reap a destiny.' The quality of attention we bring to the world establishes our habits, characters and destiny. If we change our attention, we change our destiny.*

# The Kind King and the Jealous King

*Kings often seek power, glory and fame.... and they frequently wage war for it. However sometimes they understand the only real victory one can have is over oneself. Their stories become tales of wisdom...*

The King of Koshala was famous for his generosity. He was known for being a friend of the poor and the destitute.
The King of Kashi, in the neighbouring kingdom, was sick with jealousy:
'My subjects consider him greater than I', he told his army chiefs one day. 'He has conspired to capture their hearts. Shame on him! Prepare for war. Our glory will be decided by swords.'
The battle was short. Defeated, the King of Koshala fled into the jungle.
Thereafter people saw what darkness befalls the world when the righteous suffer and justice disappears.
But the people's grief made the King of Kashi sick with anger: 'My enemy is stealing my victory. Why are they all in sorrow? Am I nothing to them? Isn't all this part of a conspiracy? Send my messengers. Let it be known throughout the country that whoever captures the King of Koshala and brings him to me will receive one hundred gold coins.'
But the people of Koshala avoided the messengers and acted as if they had heard nothing.
Isolated in the jungle, the vanquished king became an ascetic. One day a traveller asked him the way to the kingdom of Koshala.

'Why do you want to go there?' inquired the ascetic king.

The traveller told him his story:

'I was a merchant. My boat sank, leaving me penniless. I became a beggar. The King of Koshala is a friend of the poor. My misfortune will move him.'

The ascetic king smiled, concealing his desire to cry. He reflected for a while, sighed and said to the merchant:

'Come with me then, I'll take you to the one who will grant your wishes.'

Both went to the palace, entered and prostrated before the King of Kashi. The ascetic king spoke:

'Great King, I was the king of Koshala before you conquered my country. You promised one hundred gold coins to whoever brings me as a prisoner to you. King, give them to my companion, and keep your promise.'

The courtiers remained in a heavy silence. Even the soldiers had to fight their feelings to hold back their tears.

The King of Kashi did not say anything for a long while. Then suddenly he stood up laughing.

'Prisoner, do you think I could be vanquished by your death? I will not let you have any hope of that. Today, victory is mine. Oh King, take back your kingdom, and with it, take my heart also.

He took the ascetic-king by the hand, led him to the throne and placed the crown upon his dusty head.[16]

---

[16]. Rabindranath Tagore, *The golden Boat*, Jaico Publishing House, Calcutta.

## Shooting at the master

*In Asia they say 'A disciple makes a guru.'*

Fei Wei, the great archery master, had a disciple named Ki Chang. When Ki Chang had achieved near-perfection of his art, he realized he had but one rival in the world, his own teacher, Fei Wei. He therefore conceived a plan to kill him.
One day, while Fei Wei and Ki Chang were training in a field, Ki Chang shot an arrow that he aimed at his master. Fei Wei then immediately also shot one. His arrow struck the arrow of his disciple in mid flight. Ki Chan shot as many times as he had arrows, and each time Fei Wei's arrow reached and broke his disciple's arrow. But Ki Chang had one more arrow than his master. So he aimed at Fei Wei one last time. This time the master threw his javelin which broke the last arrow in full flight.
Ki Chang could only bow respectfully. Then master and disciple embraced weeping and prostrating to the ground before each other:
'Oh, great master!'
'Oh, great disciple!'[17]

[17]. Lie Tseu, Livre V, 15.

# Afraid of Tomorrow

*Anyone can be a guru-for-a-day for someone else.*

A man who lived in the suburbs of a large modern city had a great deal of anxiety about everything. He feared thieves, so he had his door reinforced. He also feared arsonists and so never left his house after dark. He was afraid of fire, was very cautious and so he had wisely taken out a good insurance policy. He also worried about accidents and so to avoid them he always refused to get a driver's license. He was terrified that he might someday develop a sickness and regularly consulted his doctor. He was worried about rain and drought, illegal immigration and unemployment, economic crises, inflation, deflation and corruption... Just about anything he could think of frightened him: hunger, cold, poverty... and death too, despite regularly attending church and doing nothing that might annoy God. For him, everything was a source of worry. He took good news as the harbinger of bad news, and bad news for the confirmation of his fears.

One day this anxious man had a fall in the street and sprained his ankle. It was nothing too serious. He was taken to the nearest doctor. The doctor gave him first aid, however he also sensed the patient's general state of anxiety. On the threshold of his consulting room, shaking his hand, he held him back a moment and said: 'Don't be afraid of tomorrow, yesterday was supposed to be just as dangerous.'

*You cannot prevent the birds of sorrow from flying over your head, but you can prevent them from building a nest in your hair, says a Chinese proverb.*

## Suffering

*Life, with its share of hardship and pains, is our teacher…*

Lawrence was the owner and manager of a thriving business. He was handsome, intelligent, cultured, courageous and determined. It seemed nothing could stand in his way. Failure and adversity was unknown to him. But he was impatient with those who were slow at understanding something, over strict with his family, curt with those who were weaker than him and he was as demanding towards others as he was towards himself.

One day his blissful world fell apart. He finally encountered fear, loneliness and vulnerability…

While he was travelling in a distant and underdeveloped country, he lost his luggage, his passport and his money. Suddenly he had nothing and was nobody.

His embassy was eight hundred miles away. How could he get there without money? He tried to call his bank manager on a reversed charges call. It was very complicated and when he finally managed to make the call, he heard that his account manager was on vacation. After several attempts a bank employee finally accepted his call, but told him he could do nothing concerning a wire transfer without a written order. Rules are rules!

Lawrence called his family and some friends. They all promised to transfer money the next day when the banks were open. But in the remote province of the country he was in, it would take several days, maybe even weeks to arrive… And with no ID how could he prove he was the recipient? What could he do?

He knew no one in this country and very few people spoke a foreign language. Each hour was bringing him closer to hunger, exhaustion and helplessness. As time passed, panic was slowly starting to set in. Where was he going to sleep that night?

He wandered the streets; the destitute were holding out their hands before him. For the first time in his life, he looked at distress with compassion. He understood what poverty, loneliness, insecurity and despair meant. He saw how his control was fragile; he realized how it was possible to be alone, abandoned and helpless.

So Lawrence did what he never imagined he would ever have to do. He noticed a rich looking shop, went in and asked to see the person in charge. The shop owner arrived with a beaming smile, thinking he would do some good business with this foreign tourist. Lawrence told him his story, his situation, how he had nothing, not even a passport and nowhere to go... He appealed to this man for help. He asked him to trust him. He was even ready to give his wedding ring as security, and his watch which was not very valuable and even the suit he was wearing.

The shop keeper interrupted him there and then, not needing to know any more. He welcomed him into his home and treated him like a friend and a brother. He offered him food, shelter, money and protection, and comforted him the best he could. What's more he refused to accept any compensation. This is how, having experienced helplessness and anguish,

Lawrence understood how compassion and generosity can overcome adversity. Thereafter, he became a more lenient and generous man.

Any painful experience is initiatory, even a burnt finger. It shakes, if not destroys, our personality. It smashes our reality, the hypnosis of our habits, and the trust in our beliefs. When we believe ourselves to be safe and beyond it all, it forces us to see that even minor events can suddenly bring us down. Through our own trials we understand the pain others experience, their fragility, and how we can learn to become more gentle, understanding and generous in our relations with them.

## Mother Teresa

*In order to be credible moral, religious, philosophical or spiritual words must resemble the acts of those who utter them.*

Mother Teresa was washing the floor, kneeling with a mop. She worked methodically without haste, her whole attention focused on the task in progress. The woman whose work had established over one hundred and sixty charity centres around the world continued to find the source of her inspiration through fulfilling the simplest of tasks as well as those which required all of her grace and intelligence.

She was very short, frail and almost lost in her white sari with blue stripes. She wore a thin smile on thin lips on a wrinkled face. Her small eyes filled with kindness expressed a grave, almost stubborn gentleness and a serene joy.

*I pay attention to one person. If I had to care for the masses I could never begin*, she used to say. Mother Teresa helped those who were in need of help. She also helped those who needed to help, inviting them to join her. She did not teach, she demonstrated by her example. To love is to act, she said. Her actions reflected her love and trying to understand it and deepen it, we imitated her. Nothing was compulsory, everything was an offering.

The actual practice of charity is what brings it to life. Mother Teresa has given charity a life through her love of her fellow man. *God loves the world through us*, she often repeated. God is the fellow man in pain that we can relieve. *Whatever you did for one of the least of these brothers of mine, you did for me.*

Thus through her the world became a friendlier place.[18]

[18]. Quotation from Matthew 24:40

## Koan

*It's important not to always try to understand and fully express the meaning of things in order to appreciate the inexpressible. Koans are good examples of this practice.*
'You know the sound of two hands clapping. What is the sound of one hand clapping?'
*According to Buddhism, man is reality itself, in its wholeness and completeness. So then, how can one exist as only a part of it? The absurdity of this situation is reflected one way or another in Koans.*
*A Koan is a form of questioning that opens the mind, giving it an opportunity to go beyond the need for a centre or coherence using questioning or doubt. They contain a sense of dilemma. In this way, a koan is a master. One can meditate on a koan for an entire life time.*
*A koan is a knot, and to untie it we have to question it relentlessly. Working on a koan is not an intellectual endeavour. It is neither a formulation of truth nor a teaching. It demands the involvement of our entire being. Therefore to work on a koan is to work on oneself, to engross oneself in it until it becomes part of oneself, until it reflects our situation perfectly, 'awakening the mind without showing it anything'. This is why the untying of a koan opens you up to an initial awakening, like a spark in a completely dark room. It awakens you to oneness, to emptiness, to the limitless void...*[19]
'Empty-handed, I carry a spade. While walking, I ride on the

[19]. Adapted from an article by Albert Low, le Troisième Millénaire, No 38.

water buffalo. I cross the bridge and there, the water does not flow, the bridge is sinking. At the top of Mount Fuji a cloud is cooking rice.'

Isan and Karin, two of Master Hyakujo's disciples, wanted to be entrusted with the mission of traveling to a place upon a beautiful mountain, south of a lake, to build a temple there. Which of the two would the master choose?
'You must decide according to the rules of Zen. You must test us with koans. The first to solve it will be chosen', said Karin.
Master Hyakujo placed a *jobin* (the bottle of water that monks carry) in front of his disciples and said:
'My dear disciples, you should not call this bottle a *jobin*. What will you call it, how else can it be described?'

(Dear reader, now try to find your own answer before reading the end of the story.)

Karin, Master Hyakujo's first disciple, replied:
'Master, I can call it a wooden sandal.'
Isan rose, took the *jobin* and poured its contents with a smile.
Master Hyakujo also smiled.[20]

---

20. *Two Zen Classics : Mumonkan and Hekiganroku*, Weatherhill, 1977.

# Killing-Blade and Life-Giving Sword

*"Look back, look out: if we meet, kill immediately! If you meet the Buddha, kill the Buddha. If you meet your ancestor, kill your ancestor! If you come across a disciple of the Buddha, kill the disciple of Buddha. If you meet your father and mother, kill father and mother! If you meet your parents, kill your parents! Only then you will find deliverance. Only then will you avoid the shackles of existence, and will you be free..."*

In the time of the Tang Dynasty, a famous priest called Nansen lived on Mount Chuan.

One day Nansen saw monks from the Eastern and Western halls quarrelling over a kitten that came to the temple. Both groups wanted to keep the animal to pamper it.

Nansen held up the cat and said:

'If you can give an answer, you will save the cat. If not, I will kill it.'

No one could answer and Nansen cut the cat in two.

That evening, Joshu, Nansen's first disciple, returned to the monastery. Nansen told him of the incident and asked his opinion.

Joshu took off his sandal, placed it on his head and walked out.

'If you had been there today, you would have saved the cat,' Nansen remarked.

*'Zen,' it is said, 'makes absolute reality through erasing appearance; and the power of true seeing lies in the knowledge that our mind has neither form nor appearance.'*

*The cute kitten probably represents beauty, or perhaps affection or attachment, or even better, the ego that must be cut... in other words appearances or mental constructions. Master Nansen embodies incisive and penetrating knowledge, and Joshu's character is certainly the expression of a wisdom that reaches beyond teaching and knowledge.*

*What could the monks have answered? They could have said three things which are true. The first: 'We are all stupid'. The second: 'The cat will be killed,' would have saved it. The third: 'Let the kitten be taken to the other hall'. Dogen Zenji suggested they could have said: 'The master knows how to cut a cat in half, but does he know how to cut in one piece?' By putting his sandal on his head, Joshu said more, he showed the formlessness of mind and the absurdity of any situation.*[21]

---

[21]. *Two Zen Classics : Mumonkan and Hekiganroku*, Weatherhill, 1977. "*Nansen cuts a cat*"; Fourteenth case. *The three true things...* are Jacques Laffitte's answers.

## The Target

*A disciple is someone who follows a discipline. No one else can do this for him...*

Ki-Chang wanted to become a disciple of Fei Wei, the great master of archery. He asked for instructions. The master said: 'First learn not to blink. Then I'll teach you archery.'

Ki-Chang returned home and trained, lying on his back under his wife's loom. He stared at the shuttle moving back and forth across the interlacing threads. His eyes became so still that a point could touch them without making him blink.

Two years had passed when he returned to Fei Wei to tell him he was ready to receive his teachings:

'Not yet,' said the master. 'Now, you need to learn to focus on a point. When, through your willpower, you can see it magnified to such an extent that you cannot miss it, then come back and I will teach you archery.'

Ki Chang hung a long horse hair at his window upon which he placed a louse to climb up it. He practiced staring at the louse even when the sun struck him in the eyes. The louse started to appear bigger and bigger to him. After three years of training in this way, through will power the louse appeared as big as a mountain to him, and he could even make out its heart. Now he could definitely hit the centre of any target.

He returned to Fei Wei and told him he was ready to receive his teachings.

'Here it is,' the master said. 'In the practice of archery the target is of no interest. If there is a goal, the goal is missed. All that matters is the quality of your gestures. And no one can teach you that. Leave, I have nothing else to teach you.'[22]

[22]. Liberally adapted from Lie Tseu ; Book V, 15.

# Habib 'Adjemi

*A disciple sometimes surpasses his master when his instructions have been applied better than the one who taught them... When the master is reminded of his own teaching, who is the master, who is the disciple, and who is wise?*

Sheikh Faroud had a disciple who followed him everywhere, drank every drop of his words, and imitated him in every way. One day, to make him understand that a master is a man like any other with their own weaknesses, Sheikh Faroud told him this story:

'Hassan, Basri, the great Sufi master, had gone on a trip. He arrived at a river bank and was trying to figure out how to cross it when Habib 'Adjemi, his former disciple also arrived there:

'O Imam of Muslims,' he said, 'what are you waiting for here?'

'I am impatiently waiting for a barge and ferryman to take me across the river.'

'O Master!' said Habib, 'I was y our student and your disciple for many years. You have taught me science and religion. You taught me to chase immoderate desires, passion and greed out of heart and this chase love of this world out of it. You taught me if ordeals arise, consider them good fortune. Finally, whatever may happen to remember that the Almighty Lord sends it to you, then, put foot on the water and cross to the other side.'

And no sooner had he finished speaking than he set foot on

the river and went across… swimming.

What I expect from you is not blind submission,' added Sheikh Faroud, 'but penetrating lucidity, because you also have things to teach me.'[23]

[23]. The story told by Cheikh Faroud was transmitted by Farid-ud-Dun'Attar.

## The Pandit

*'Words are mere symbols to express truth. But confusing words with truth is just as misleading as confusing the finger that points to the moon with the moon itself.'* [24]

One day, a pandit went to see the king in his palace and said: 'My Lord, I know the Scriptures well. I would like to teach you the words of our Gods and the wisdom of our rishis.'
The king knew that a man who has really studied and accomplished the Scriptures would seek solitude and contemplation rather than the wealth and honour of the court. He answered the pandit:
'I see you have not yet quiet understood the ultimate meaning of religion and philosophy. I promise to take you as my tutor, but keep on studying the word of the Gods and the secrets of the sages.'
The pandit returned home, very upset. How could anyone say that he had not yet understood when he knew all the scriptures and the most complicated rituals by heart! However, he resumed his studies and returned to the palace a few years later. The king repeated what he had said the first time and sent him back. Extremely upset, the Pandit returned home and continued studying the scriptures. Gradually, the hidden meanings of the written words became apparent to his mind. He gave up the world and renounced pleasures, devoting himself to the quest for perfection. He understood the futility of

[24]. *The teaching of Buddha*, Bukkyo Dendo Kyokai, Tokyo, Japan, 1979.

royal courts, the worthlessness of wealth and the vanity of honours, and thought of the king no more.

A few years later, the king remembered the pandit and went to visit him. He found him in a solitary hut at the very end of the city, living in extreme poverty. Seeing him radiating with the divine lights of love, peace and joy, he knelt before him and said:

'I see you have really understood the Scriptures, if you will accept me as your disciple, I am ready to become one.'[25]

---

[25]. Adapted from a Hindu tale: *Tales of immortal India*, Sattia Publishing, Patna.

## The cup

*Sometimes the disciple is unaware he has reached the end of his apprenticeship. He doesn't realize he has equalled his master. He must then complete the last stage of his initiation: leave the master to become a maser in his own right.*

Shanta Puri yogi and his disciple Ananda lived together in the jungle for many years. Ananda was devoted to his guru and attentive to his teachings. 'When shall I finally attain wisdom?' he sometimes wondered.

One day, the yogi decided to send him away:

'I taught you all I know. I have nothing more to teach you. Now go.'

'Master, where shall I go? I still know almost nothing. Let me stay with you,' Ananda pleaded.

'Go to the lord of this kingdom. He is a great initiate and his wisdom is famous. He alone can guide you now.'

Obedient to his master, our man went through the jungle, walked from village to village until one day he came to the town and then the royal palace.

That day, a great feast was given in honour of the queen. The man was taken to the magnificent palace reception hall where all the kingdom's dignitaries and hundreds of guests had gathered and were drinking, eating, laughing and dancing before the king and the queen sitting on their thrones. Ananda made his way through the crowd, and then eventually bowed down three times at the feet of his new master with reverent humility before addressing the king:

'Majesty, I was a disciple of Shanta Puri yogi for fourteen years. My guru told me he had nothing more to teach me and sent me to you. Only you, he said, can now take me beyond and even beyond the beyond.

The king smiled at Ananda, then, with a simplicity that combined wisdom and love, he handed him a cup filled to the brim:

'Take it, carry it around the room and bring it back to me without spilling a single drop.'

Going round this hall which was full of the bustle and commotion of a crowd of drinking and agitated people, how could he avoid bumping into anyone? How could he keep the necessary stability amongst all this turmoil? The test seemed impossible. But Ananda had learned to obey his gurus whatever their orders; he was able to go beyond his fears and transform the impossible into the possible.

He took the cup from the king's hands and advanced slowly through the crowd of guests, evenly paced, perfectly focused, practicing acute vigilance as his past guru had taught him, making himself one with the cup, its content and the reception hall.

An hour later he found himself back at the feet of the king. He handed him the nectar filled cup without one single drop missing. Amazed the king took it, drank it, thanked his disciples and said:

'I have nothing to teach you either.'[26]

---

[26]. Adapted from a tale found in the wisdom of India and in the Tibetan Buddhist teachings

# The man who knew the secret of immortality

*Some know but can't. Others don't know but they could if they knew....*

In times past, a man claimed to have knowledge of the Tao of immortality. The prince of Yen heard about him and sent one of his ministers to find him and bring him back. However it took so long to find this man in possession of the Tao of immortality that he died before the ministers could convey the prince's invitation. Chi Tzu also wanted to know the Tao of immortality. When he found out that the man who held that science died, he was very distressed.

Master Fu-tzu heard about this and laughed:

'This man has lost his own life,' he said. 'How could he possibly have saved you from death?'

Hearing these words, Hou-tzu remarked:

'Fu-tzu's words are empty.' And he told this story:

'A man from the province of Wei became an outstanding calculator. He was very old. Before he died, he passed his knowledge on to his son. The son could remember the words of his father perfectly but he could not perform the calculations. One day a man asked the son to repeat to him the knowledge his father gave him. As a result he became a calculator who was just as brilliant as the old man.

Hou-tzu said: 'Some men have the methods but are not able to put them into practice. On the other hand, some men have the ability to put them into practice if only they knew the methods.'[27]

[27]. Adapted from Lie tseu, Foreign Languages Press, Beijing..

# III

## Religions and People

*Why do we get so uptight about our own religion? Did those who transmitted it to us, know God or were they, like us, simply attached to their family traditions? Did our fathers never endure war, pain and misfortune? Were they any closer to God, or to the truth, than the fathers of the Babylonians, the ancient Greeks, the people of Pharaonic Egypt, the Incas, the Yanomamis, the Aborigines, the native Americans? Did they receive any better answers to their prayers?*
*For thousands of years men have been asking themselves the same questions about life, what precedes it and what follows it. Spiritual and metaphysical response are what shape religions. They are available to us. We can use them. Knowing about them is certainly a good thing, because the ideas and methods that we can learn from other traditions enrich and clarify our own inherited tradition.*
*Everything is God! Nothing is God! God is neither in the world nor outside the world! Do these conflicting statements all reveal some truth? 'From the point of view of form, everything is other than God; from the point of view of truth everything is none other than Him,' said Djami, the Sufi poet.*

*'Knowing that I am nothing is wisdom. Knowing that I am everything is love. Between wisdom and love, there is my life,' taught Shree Nisargadatta Maharaj.*

*What do the wise say about religions? Do they lead us to peace? Do they make us wise? Do they turn us towards love? Do they tell us the truth?*

## Faith and Duty

One day, Faith met Duty.
'Do you believe in what you do?' asked the first one.
'Do you act according to what you believe in?' retorted the other.
Faith without action is merely a figment of imagination, and duty without reasoned understanding is mere alienation. From the futility of the debate between them arose the justification not to believe in anything and not to do anything but seek wisdom as the sole goal.
That which lies between faith and blind faith, religion and atheism, is not simply nothingness. Doubt may be productive and a measure of faith as well. Knowledge exists to guide our intelligence; whilst gurus explain, demonstrate and inspire us.[28]

[28]. Adapted liberally from a saying of Shri Bhagavan Aryadeva, *Words of the guru*, Lotus/Chou, Paris, 1980.

## Lost in the jungle

Once upon a time, there was a hunter lost in the jungle. For three days, he wandered alone without finding his way and without even encountering anyone to ask. He was in need of food and slept with one eye open, fearing wild beasts and snakes.

He was just starting to get panic when, on the morning of the fourth day, he saw a man sitting under a tree, just like him. He ran over to him and embraced him. They were both overjoyed.

'I was lost,' said the former to the latter.

'Me too,' said the other.

They both discovered they were lost. Buth now they found they both were lost together.

Faith often brings lost people together who would like to believe that they are less lost when there are several of them who are lost together. They think that if there are many of them believing in something, then this thing must be true. Just as two mad men are not equal to one wise one, two errors do not make a truth, and one thousand believers do not sum up to authentic knowledge.[29]

*Faith is a means to an end; it is a path but not a goal or an end in itself.*

*Believing sometimes means you are certain and then sometimes it means you are not completely sure but that you*

[29]. Adapted from a Hindu traditional tale.

*have an inclination. When someone says 'I believe' it is an affirmation which contains the ambiguity of certainty and doubt. There* is conviction and adherence but not knowledge and experience.

*Faith gives an emotional and an irrational bias to a view making it a position that is not established by proof but rather by desire or hope. Creeds, our definitive affirmations, are a refusal to acknowledge that faith has nothing to do with truth, that belief is an attempt to fill the void of ignorance with something other than knowledge.*

## The sacrifice

*The Buddha said 'Be your own support and your own refuge, find refuge in yourself and no one else. Do not believe in anything simply because it is written in religious books. Do not accept anything without examination. It is your own responsibility to make the effort towards liberation.'*[30]

A hermit was living in the heart of the jungle, far from the trials and tribulations of normal life. He believed he would find enlightenment in solitude and renunciation. He had taken Agni for his chosen God and worshiped fire uninterruptedly, feeding a bonfire and singing praises continuously for several years. However one day, he noticed that nothing in him had changed, he felt no closer to God or more awakened than at the beginning of his asceticism.

He decided to sacrifice everything in the hope that his God would finally appear and reveal the eternal secrets to him.

His only possession was a buffalo and yet he resolved to sacrifice it.

He took a purification bath and built an altar of logs and branches according to the ancient prescriptions. However he didn't have a blade of darbha, the sacred grass, so he tied up the animal and went up the mountain to search for it.

During his absence, some hunters discovered his buffalo and took it away with them. When the hermit returned, he saw

[30]. Fragments from Dhammapada, XII, 4; VII, 8; XX, 4; then Mahâparinirvana sûtra.

that his buffalo was missing, he discovered the hunters tracks and he understood:
'Oh, God of fire, I was wasting my time! How can I continue to worship your power, when you cannot even look after what is yours?'
So the man gave up worshipping, rituals and sacrifices and devoted himself to the pursuit of knowledge.

*Don't try to question silence because silence cannot speak; don't expect anything from praying to Gods; don't try to bribe them with sacrifices; one must search for liberation in oneself - the Buddha.*[31]

---

[31]. Adapted from Bouddha Jataka : *History of Buddhism*, Keisai, 1976, Tokyo. The Jâtaka, Low Price Publications, Delhi.

# The elephant

Pratap had a deep and sincere faith in God. He said he saw God in everyone, in everything and everywhere…

One day, as he was going to the temple, a man came running toward him shouting:

'Beware! A mad elephant is running this way. It's crushing everything. Get out of here!'

Other passersby took to their heels, but Pratap thought that this elephant was a manifestation of God. Why, then, should he run away from God? He stood in the middle of the road, and prostrated himself waiting for it.

The man, who was the mahout, warned him again:

'Run away! Hide somewhere!'

But Pratap did not budge.

The elephant soon arrived with heavy steps shaking the earth and the trees all around. Without even slowing its pace, it seized Patrap in his trunk, threw him on the side and went its way.

Pratap was lying unconscious. Wounded and bruised, he was taken home. When he awoke, Ramlal swami asked him:

'You knew that a mad elephant was coming, why did you not flee like everyone else?'

'God is everywhere; he takes animal and human forms, so I thought that God was manifesting in the form of an elephant.'

'Of course everything is a manifestation of God. The mad elephant-God was coming your way but the mahout-God told you not to stay there. Why didn't you listen to the manifestation of God that was warning you?'[32]

---

32 . Adapted from *Tales of immortal India*, Sattia Publishings, Patna. Also told by Ramakrishna in *The Gospel of Sri Râmakrishna*, swami Nikkhilananda ; Ramakrishna-Vivekananda Center; New-York; 1992

## Lost

*All, visible and invisible, that exists in Him, with Him, apart from Him, is not other than He, for the other itself is He, said Ibn 'Arabi.*[33] *And therefore the one who seeks God is God himself; God is himself the seeker, and for that reason he is the one who is lost and bewildered is as well, replied the bewildered one.*

Two hermits, one wise and one mad, lived not far apart in the forest. One day, the mad one paid a visit to the wise one.

'Who are you?' asked the wise to the mad.

'I am you,' declared the mad man. 'And you, who are you?'

'What I know is that I don't know,' the wise replied. 'I'm here to try and find out.'

'Well, me neither, I don't know who I am,' said the mad one logically. 'What are you doing here?'

'I'm seeking God.'

'So am I' replied the mad one. 'How do you do it?'

'I believe the world is not real. I observe this belief.'

'As for me, I see the madness of the world. It probably amounts to the same thing since I'm crazy.'

'Although you do not seem to be aware of it you appear to be quite wise. So how did this all happen? How did we end up here looking for God?' asked the wise to the mad.

And the mad told him the following story:

In the beginning, God created the world, and then he con-

33. *What the Seeker Needs,* Muhyiddin Ibn 'Arabi.

ceived and formed all sorts of living beings. Then he declared that everything he had done was fine and beautiful, and he was very pleased. But when he tried to return from whence he came from, God realized he could no longer find the way back to heaven. He was lost and bewildered. And he also noticed that his might was rapidly declining.

He took the form of a sparrow, and asked a swallow:

'What is the way to God?'

'Fly and you'll be in heaven!' she answered gliding along through the sky.

But the sky above the ground was not God's abode.

He took the form of a mole and questioned a worm in the same way.

'God is in the earth. Dig and you'll see him,' the worm told him, swallowing a mouthful of earth.

But the earth under the ground was not the abode of God either.

He plunged into the water and met a small goldfish:

'Do you know who you are and where you come from?' God asked him.

'I don't know who I am or where I come from,' replied the fish. 'But I believe that God created me and that he is everywhere just like the water that I swim in and from where I breathe.

'If God is everywhere, how can you find him?'

'This too I don't know. But when I spin round and round, I feel that God is very close to me.'

This fish is a fool, thought God, or maybe he is mad…

'You don't know who you are and where you come from, and

yet you believe that God created you! If he made you so ignorant, he must be just the same. Do you think that God believes in God?' God said bursting out laughing.
He left the fish, returned on dry land and took the form of a snake. He met a huge elephant.
'I am God,' declared the elephant.
God looked at this creature and thought: if this is God, who am I?
The elephant then added gravely:
'I am God, just like you, lost in life, unable to find the way back to where I was before.
'Do you think there is a way? Can something or someone help us?'
'I'm not sure, but I carry on searching.'
So God realized that everything he had created was like him, lost in the world and in life. He left the elephant, and wandered on earth. One day, he met a large, old turtle who lived like a hermit on the seashore. God told her his story; he confessed that he had created this world and now could not find the way back to himself.
'How can I find the path to God?' asked God.
'To find out that path I have renounced the world,' the turtle replied, already drawing in her neck into her shell.
Having heard these words, God knew he too had to renounce the world if he wanted to find himself. But deep in himself, he discovered that he did not want to renounce the world…
'Is there no other way?' he asked the turtle.
So the turtle slowly peaked her nose out of her shell to say:
'You are the causeless Being and the cause of being. So try to

find some purpose for being.'

God then took some earth and formed it into the shape that men call 'man.' He then breathed himself into it. He hasn't given up seeking a way to heaven. And he is still looking for one.

# What kind of religion?

*Whoever wants to convert others to his faith first has to present them with reasons to believe. These often consist of fears, anxieties, fascinations and dark imaginings. A sage never shares his faith, only his experience.*

A priest was heard preaching to a nonbeliever:
'You must work for your salvation, adopt the true religion, obey the laws of God, pray the way it has been taught, love thy neighbour and practice charity just as the Scriptures have taught us, and you must believe in eternal life after death. Otherwise, come Judgment Day, you will have bitter regrets.'
The nonbeliever replied:
'I'll never be able to emulate the courage and asceticism of the saints, and I'll never have the wisdom of the wise men I respect. If you're referring to your own faith, I have no desire in sharing it, for, anyone who might otherwise be drawn towards God will inevitably lose interest in him by seeing you. Your faith is nothing but a string of threats and obligations. It's as if you are calling for people to find love in the desert, discover kindness in fear, seek happiness under duress, confuse life with death, mistake wisdom for faith and obedience, and finally consider God to be an investment…'[34]

[34]. Adapted very liberally from a Sufi story of which variants can be found in Farid-ud-Dun'Attar; in Djalâl al-Dîn Rûmî, *The Essential Rumi*, translation by Colman Barks, John Meyne, 1997 ; and in Indries Shah, *Tales of the Dervishes*, Vicking Penguin ; 1972.

## The conference

One day, during an interfaith conference which brought together delegates from five major faiths, a person in the audience asked this question:
'Why do Jews celebrate on Saturday, Christians on Sunday and Muslims on Friday?'
The rabbi replied:
'Jews celebrate on Saturday, because they believe that God created the world in six days, the seventh day, the first Saturday of Creation, he ceased to create it and intervened no more with creative acts. God left the world to mankind. Jews celebrate this gift.'
The priest said:
'Christians believe Jesus-Christ to be the son of God who came to save people from sins. That's why they celebrate on Sunday, the eighth day of Creation, the first day of a new time, the Good News era.'
The imam quoted his scriptures:
"When God decided something it was determined by him, and having determined it, he inscribed it in the Book, and it is in accordance with this Book that he created all beings and governs their life". For Muslims, the world is still in the duration of the sixth day of Creation, because God has not withdrawn from the world and continues to govern it. Everything that happens manifests his desire and his almighty will. That's why we celebrate on Friday, the day God created Man on earth.'
In turn, the lama spoke:

'We don't know if God created the world, if this world was created in six days, and if it is better to celebrate on Friday, Saturday or Sunday. We know that this world contains suffering. The question is how can we free ourselves from it? We believe that we must be equally and simultaneously detached and attentive to every day, every hour, every minute, because we celebrate life in a human body of which every moment offers an opportunity to understand suffering and be liberated from it.'

The Swami meditated for a moment and then whispered:

'If God created the world, isn't everything in this world and beyond holy? But is there a real world? Or is this world but a dream, an illusion, a mirage? We celebrate the Moon, the Sun and the Earth, we worship husband, wife and child, we glorify fasting and fasting, we honour God the Creator, the God who preserves and the destroyer God, life and death, we extol the virtues of wisdom, devotion, knowledge, love and charity... We bless and sanctify everything, everyday in cvcry moment.'

Then the moderator closed the session saying:

'Sharing our questions is easier than sharing our answers, for our answers are different, but our questions are the same.'[35]

[35]. The imam quote : Kuran 22: 10

# The blessed city

*Living according to one's beliefs is wisdom, they say. But taking the precepts of religion at face value could be as saintly or as madness....*

In his youth, Gibran was told that in a certain city every one lived according to the Scriptures. And he said, 'I will seek that city and the blessedness thereof.' It was far away, so he made great provisions for his journey. After forty days of travelling he beheld the city, and on the forty-first day he entered it.
Upon arriving, lo and behold! In the whole company of the inhabitants each had but a single eye and but one hand. He was astonished and said to himself, 'Is it possible that in such a holy city everyone has but one eye and one hand?"
Then he saw that they too were astonished, for they were marvelling greatly at his two hands and two eyes. As they were speaking together, he inquired of them saying, 'Is this indeed the Blessed City, where every man lives according to the Scriptures?' And they said, 'Yes, this is that very city.'
'But what has befallen you,' he said. 'Where are your right eyes and your right hands?'
All the people were moved and they said to him, 'Come and see.'
So they took him to the temple in the midst of the city. Inside the temple he saw a heap of hands and eyes, all withered and dry. Then he said: 'Alas! What conqueror has committed this cruelty upon you?'
Then a murmur went amongst them. Finally one of their elders

came forth and said, 'This is our own doing. God has made us conquerors over the evil that was in us.'

And he led him to a high altar, and all the people followed. And he showed Gibran a graven inscription above the altar which read:

'If your right eye causes you to sin, tear it out and throw it away. For it is better for you to lose one part of your body than for your whole body to go into hell. And if your right hand causes you to sin, cut it off and throw it away. For it is better that you lose one of your members than that your whole body be thrown into hell.'

Then Gibran understood and turned about to all the people and cried, 'Has no man or woman among you two eyes or two hands?'

And they answered him saying, 'No, not one. There is none, save those who are yet too young to read the Scripture and to understand its commandment.'

Upon leaving the temple, Gibran left the Blessed City immediately; for he was not too young, and he was able to read the scripture.[36]

---

[36]. Gibran, *The Madman*, Alfred Knopf, 1949. Quote for the Gospel: Matthew 5, 29.

# The camel fair

Sheikh Assam told me this story:
'A man felt that he needed a camel so he went to the fair and spoke with the cattle breeders:
"See how mine is strong, look how powerful it is," said the first one, "it will carry all your burdens and your worries with it!"
"You need a hardy camel," said another, "a camel who will live a long time and will take you far away!"
"O Sahib, take this camel covered with gold and honours," said the third, 'with this one you will be received at the Caliph's court."
"An old camel is what you need," said yet another. "This one has breathed the dust of all the roads and has acquired wisdom."
"Mine eats little and it can read and count!"
"The king himself rode upon this one!"
"The great-great-grandfather of mine saw the Prophet..."
O friend, religion is like a camel fair,' Sheikh Assam explained. 'Priests, saints, prophets and their cousins offer you their religion; they promise you eternal life, heaven, happiness, knowledge... What do they want you to give for it? Obedience? Subordination? Can they themselves walk without a mount?
If what you seek is God, you have no need of a camel nor of a religion. God is not far from you. God is something of a solitary affair. He is within you; you can talk about it, but you cannot share it or sell it. You must go by yourself. And on your way, listen to those who are free, and run as fast as you can away from those who want to take hold of your freedom,' concluded the Sufi master.[37]

---

[37]. Cheikh Assam, in Patrick Levy, *Dieu croit-il en Dieu ?* Albin Michel/ Question de; Paris, 1993.

# The Babri mosque

*'The reasons men may have to hate or love one another are infinite,' J.L. Borges.*

One day, over a hundred years ago, a Muslim man prayed in the Babri mosque in Ayodhya, India, and he had a vision of Ram, the Hindu God. A miracle!

The fact that Ram, one of the ten avatars of Vishnu, appeared not to a Hindu but to a Muslim was an extraordinary event. Moreover this happening in a mosque rather than in a Hindu temple was amazing news. It would open the way to numerous interpretations, expressions of love, of hate and a great deal of suffering. Nearly one hundred years later some Hindus decreed that the Babri mosque had been built where there was once, centuries ago, a temple dedicated to Ram, and furthermore that this temple indicated the birthplace of this avatar.

The Ramayana says that Ram was born in Ramjanmabhoomi. However it is far from certain that this town was situated in the same place as today's Ayodhya, and that Ram was therefore born there.

Those with a profound love of God understood the manifestation of Ram to a Muslim as an invitation to tolerance, a reminder of our brotherhood in humanity over faith and a symbol of divine unity: 'God is One, His ways are unforeseen and for him everything is possible', these people said, whether Hindus or Muslims.

But the fierce believers in a single truth, those who believe in last revelations or unquestioned faith rejected these attitudes. 'There is but one God only, his name is Allah, and Muhammad is his last prophet. He is not associated with any other. There is no other God, nothing is beyond him and nothing happens without his will,' they proclaimed. 'If the Islamic warriors have conquered India,' they argued, 'it was because Allah-the-Almighty willed it. Furthermore Allah also willed the revelation of the aberration of Hindu customs and beliefs. Therefore, if Ram appeared to a Muslim in a mosque, it could only mean one thing: Islam is the last revelation, replacing all the old traditions.'

Of course, the most zealous Hindus did not see it like that at all. 'If Ram manifested to a Muslim in a mosque, obviously he was showing that Islam was a mistake, and was indicating the right path. Moreover, if Muslims had invaded India and Ram had given them victory, it was so that Muslims could receive Ram's revelation!' They decided to destroy the Babri mosque erected on the supposed birthplace of Ram, and rebuild a Hindu temple on the site. Of course this project succeeded in raising tensions, unrest, anger, fighting and death.

Everyone saw the miracle of Ram's manifestation through the filter of his own belief. Everyone saw it as evidence for their own faith, and took it as a cause for hostility, rejection or appeasement.

What was the difference between the Muslim fundamentalists and the Hindu fanatics? They were both looking for reasons to fight, so in this they were both very similar. They claimed their religions were different, but both of these faiths led them to act in the same way! Both of their faiths inspired hatred in them.

# The Marquise

During the nineteenth century in Northern Italy most people practiced their Roman Catholic religion, going to church diligently, confessing regularly and trying to be scrupulous in following rules of good conduct and morality.

In the churches, they repeated a creed which contained this sentence: 'I believe in Jesus Christ who was conceived by the Holy Ghost and born of the Virgin Mary...'

One day in a city of this country, the Marquise of M. discovered she was pregnant. This was all the more puzzling since she had never known a man, absolutely never. She called the doctor, who confirmed it, then the midwife also corroborated the doctor's diagnosis. She was pregnant!

Rumours spread the news of the Marquise's pregnancy. And when she assured people that she had never had relations with a man, no one believed her. She was condemned without mercy. Her own mother doubted her sincerity, her father sent her away from home. There was not a single good soul in the city who would give the Marquise the benefit of the doubt.

As for us, how can we tell whether the Marquise had known a man or not. What we do know is that the inhabitants of this city could believe in Jesus Christ, conceived by the Holy Spirit and born of the Virgin Mary... They could accept an amazing event as being true as long as it was supposed to have happened far away and long ago, and furthermore proclaimed by religious authorities. But in their own lifetime and close to home, they refused to believe that the laws of nature could be disturbed by miracles.

These good people who regularly prayed to Jesus and Mary were probably just like those who, long ago, condemned Jesus Christ. Human nature had not changed. So are we amongst those who turn away from a saint or amongst those who become his disciples?'

Judge not so that you will not be judged. Let he who is without sin cast the first stone...'[38]

[38]. La Marquise d'O. by Heinrich von Kleist. Matthew 7: 1; John 8: 7

# Guilty or not guilty, that is the question

*If God wants to prevent evil and never can, he is powerless;*
*If he can and does not want to, he is perverse;*
*If he neither can nor wants to, he is powerless and perverse;*
*If he wants to and can, why doesn't he do it?*

*Epicurus.*

Whilst life can be exciting, it is also often difficult and frightening.
Ten thousand years ago, our ancestors became aware of this. Life is cruel and painful but what could they do with this simple truth, this blunt and obvious awareness? They could do next to nothing. They found themselves limited by their powerlessness.
They invented Gods, gave them attributes and prayed to them. But the Gods didn't sympathize with the hardships of mankind. Despite their rituals, invocations and sacrifices, people still had accidents and enemies and were struck with drought and disease. Their prayers to every imaginable God hardly changed anything.
So they started looking for causes: if the Gods refused to alleviate life's hardships, they were probably responsible for their hardships. They were guilty of something. They had sinned...
This is how our ancestors conceived the guilt of being alive.
This was to become the foundation of religions. The Yanomamis had fallen from the Big Tree and they were waiting for the

gods to call them back; the Giziga had pushed away the sky which fed them; Adam, the first man, disobeyed God's order of things by eating the fruit from the tree of knowledge of good and evil; Karma is the cause of birth. Actions from past lives cause this present birth. But what was the cause of karma? What caused the first act, before there was any former act? Everyone thought it was important to regain purity. Everyone believed they had to try to erase the catastrophic event which had caused life to be miserable and dangerous.

For this, they conceived all kinds of taboos, prohibitions, rules of good conduct, regulations concerning hair and clothing; some forbid themselves pleasures, others mutilated themselves, others devoted their life to fasting and mortification. Life was hard, so in atoning for their sins and regaining the imaginary original innocence, paying for the ontological guilt of being with pain, they made it even harder.

But the gods still refused to relieve mankind of its misery and hardships. They didn't alleviate suffering nor did they prevent misfortune, either because they were powerless to, or because the burden of sin and guilt was even greater than imagined. However, few imagined that the Gods could do nothing about it.

Since then, we haven't changed much. Some have reduced the Gods to one, but continue on despising life by cursing it with guilt. And we maintain the belief in a before when things were better.

How can you still conceive a powerful, providential, merciful, fatherly God after the Deluge, the Holocaust, Hiroshima, and many other individual and collective disasters? Each hardship invites us to reconsider what we think of God and Providence, or pushes us a little further towards guilt. Because if we keep on believing that a kind God governs the world, we logically have to assign the responsibility of pain and hardship to the one experiencing it. Or even worse believe that a victim is more guilty than a killer. Worse still drawing the logical conclusion that the killer is the arm of God.

The reality of life's ups and downs will not change, or it would already have changed. If we want to change something, let's try to be kind.

Since the beginning of time, we suffer and try to find a reason for this suffering. We have invented the guilt of being and made Gods responsible for misfortune and happiness. But we have also invented love and pleasure and we have extended them out into altruism and compassion. Thus the harshness of life can be transformed into mercy, compassion, solidarity, prevention, relief.

## Who has seen God?

*Those who claim that God exists have not seen him. They have not met anyone who has seen him or even someone who knows someone who has seen him...*

'Tell me, Vâssettha,' the Buddha asked his disciple, 'has any one Brahmin among all of the Brahmins versed in the Vedas ever seen God personally, face to face?'

'No, venerable Gotama, there are none.'

'Now tell me Vâssettha, has any one teacher of the Brahmins among all the teachers of the Brahmins versed in the Vedas ever seen God personally, face to face?'

'No, there is none, venerable Gotama.'

'Tell me again Vassettha, did the Rishis of the Brahmins versed in the Vedas, or the authors of the Vedas or of the incantations in which the old forms of words are sung, ever say: "We know who God is. We know where he came from and where he is going.'

'No, they never said such a thing, venerable Gotama.'

'Yet, the Brahmins who are proclaiming: 'Here is the direct path, the path of salvation, the one leading to the state of union with God', are in fact saying: 'We are demonstrating the path of union with someone of whom we know nothing, whom we have not seen'. If we look at the facts, aren't the Brahmins' words foolish?'

'Yes, definitely, venerable Gotama.'

'Suppose, Vâsettha, that a man says: "I am waiting for the most beautiful girl in this country and I wish to marry her." One might ask him: "Do you know her caste, her family name? Do you know what village she lives in? Is she tall or short, black, brown, or golden?" Questioned in this way, he replies that he doesn't know. Wouldn't anyone then say to him: "Well, you're waiting for a girl that you don't know!" Therefore, is it possible for the Brahmins to show the path of union with someone they know nothing of and have not seen?'
'Certainly not, venerable Gotama.'
'Suppose, Vâsettha, that a man should come hither to the bank of the river wishing to cross, to reach the other side. Imagine then that the man standing on the bank invokes the river bank on the other side saying, "Come here, O other side! Come to this side!" Do you suppose, Vâsettha, that because of the invocations, prayers, wishes and praises of this man, the other river bank actually comes to his side?'
'Certainly not, venerable Gotama.'
'Similarly, Vâsettha, is it possible that the Brahmins, because of their invocations, prayers, wishes and praises, are able to unite with God?'[39]

*'Who knows, who could proclaim for sure from whom this creation was born and from whence it came? Gods were born after the creation of our world. But who knows where*

[39].Tevijja-Sûtra, *sermon of the Bouddha.*

*the world comes from? Whoever it is that watches over this world from the highest heavens can only know. Or maybe he does not.' Rig Veda*[40]

[40]. Rig Veda 10 :129.

## Give them knowledge

*'A religion has less to fear in its critics than from within itself, especially when it has lost what it wanted to hide,' - Aryadeva.*

In the U.S., the Dalai Lama had been invited to address a gathering of American Jews. At the end of his lecture, someone asked him this question:
'How can we prevent our children from converting to Buddhism?'
The Dalai Lama replied:
'If you have knowledge, you must give it to them. If you don't have it, then you can't prevent them from going to look for it.'

# IV

## The Other Religion

*In the West as well as in the East, indeed everywhere, there are two religions within every religion. There is mainstream religion, called faith. This consists of dogmas, a one-size-fits-all creed, that is a kind of ready-to-wear for religious thought and feeling. Then there is the mystic's or the wise man's religion, which may also be called spirituality. This consists of methods and practices that lead one to know something, to experience a different relationship with the world and beyond.*

*In the mystical traditions, the pinnacle of the spiritual quest is union with the One. Meister Eckhart, twelfth century Catholic from the Rhineland said: 'Simple people imagine that they must see God as if he were there and they were here. It's not so. God and I are One in knowledge. The person who knows and that which is known are One.'*

*God is One. We emphasize this One with a capital letter. So does this mean there is only one God rather than several? Or does it rather mean that which is One, unified, is divine?*

*For, if God is One, can he be 'other' or 'different'? Aren't 'One' and 'other' incompatible? If God was someone or something 'different' (he is also sometimes called the "radically different"), then within the very heart of his faith and his attempt to become One, the man who is faithful to this God will remain in a duality consisting of the believing subject, the 'I', and the object of faith, God. So that by calling upon, or searching the sole 'One', he would still be rooted in a state of separation. If God is One, are we not that very God and wouldn't knowledge of that God be accessible within ourselves? Isn't this the meaning of monotheism - the quest for this sole One?*

*God is either different from us, meaning we must have faith or give up searching, or God is not different, in which case we have to ask spiritual questions: Where is God in me? What is divine in man? In what way are God and man different? How are they similar?*

*All religious traditions have both taught a God who is 'other' and a God within man. Religious creeds speak of a different God; mystics bear witness of God within themselves and teach the paths that lead to knowing or getting close to him. What matters then is to learn to 'see' God or to see like God, or to join him in silence. The important thing is to increase our awareness and intimacy of this God within, in the way we see the world.*

# Abraham

*It isn't faith that makes someone a prophet, but the fact that he somehow hears God, he knows God. He establishes a direct and personal relationship with him.*

Terah, Abraham's father, was the possessive and powerful chief of a tribe of several hundred shepherds who lived in the land of Ur, in Chaldea. He was a polytheist and idol worshipper.

Of course, Abraham showed respect and obedience to his father, but deep down he longed to be emancipated from him. Yet how could he leave his tribe without weakening it? How could he abandon his father without damaging or wearing down his authority? How could he convince him to let him leave, with a few men and a portion of the flock? Only a higher power would allow it.

He was meditating on this for a long time when he had a revelation: he heard *Lekh lekha*, in Hebrew, as a godly command coming from the depths of his inner being, 'Go to yourself.'

When Terah asked him why he wanted to go, Abraham replied:

'A God told me to leave.'

'A God? Which God?'

'The Only God.'

How could Terah oppose this? He himself obeyed the gods? He let him go.

'Go to yourself,' the first words the Only God spoke to the

man who would become the father of monotheism, is the original meaning of religion: the spiritual guidance for man and the object of his quest. Going towards oneself to be united, to be One, in the image and likeness of God. The God of Abraham didn't tell him: 'come to me', for there is no way to get there except through yourself.[41]

*'To seek wisdom, leave brothers, country, friends and family,' said Epictetus.*

[41]. Geneses 12:1. God said to Abraham : *Lekh leka*, which Rachi translates "Go to yourself".

# Râmakrishna

*There are many religions and within each one there are numerous different sects. Some religions arose from religions which already existed and their relevance is sometimes referred to in the new one. Jesus, the founding figure of Christianity, was a Jew. Buddha was a Hindu... 'Had Allah willed, He could have made you one congregation. But He thus puts you to the test through the revelations He has given each of you.'*[42]

'Men draw the boundaries of their fields using barriers and markers,' taught Ramakrishna, 'but no one can limit the vast and indivisible sky extending over our heads, around us which includes us all.

A man who has not received enlightenment says, in his ignorance, that his religion is the best and the only true one. But when his heart has been enlightened by true knowledge, he realizes that what we understand about God is only what God himself makes us understand, and that beyond all the quarrels and creeds of the sects, there is but only one absolute Being-Knowledge-Bliss.

Just as one can get to the roof of a house using a ladder, a bamboo, a staircase, a rope, or various other means, ways and paths to reach God are many. Every religion shows us a path to reach him. All religions lead to God, but the paths are not God.

The Scriptures indicate a direction. Once you know the way,

[42]. Koran 5: 48.

put down the holy books and try to reach the goal.[43]

*That's what Serapion, one of the Desert Fathers, did. He sold his Gospel book and gave the money to the hungry, saying:*
*'I sold the book which instructed me to distribute all my belongings to the poor.'*[44]

[43]. *The Gospel of Sri Râmakrishna*, Swami Nikkhilananda ; Râmakrishna-Vivekananda Center; New-York; 1942.
[44]. Quotation by Thomas Merton, *The Wisdom of the Desert.*

## Djihad

*If God is as powerful as they say he is, he certainly has no need of anyone to fight for him. Those who still believe that waging war for God is a sign of heroism would do better to defeat their desires with the same ardour. Serenity sometimes requires more courage than the fiercest of battles...*[45]

A Sufi man had fought naked, in ninety wars without any protection, hoping to find death in the service of God. He had received severe beatings, spear, sword and arrow wounds, but none of his injuries had ever been life threatening.
'Having been deprived of the joy of martyrdom,' he said, 'alone in a cave, I withdrew from the world. One day, I heard the sound of drums: soldiers were going to war. I felt an intense excitement throughout my entire being: 'Get up, now is the time to fight. Fulfil your wish to become a martyr in a war.'
But my soul replied:
'What is the reason for hiding behind this ruse O devious ego? You want to die in battle because the thing you most fear is the efforts of asceticism and the throes of austerity!'
'O my soul, here, no one knows of the ordeals and defeats that you put me through,' said my ego. 'If I could die in combat, then at least everyone would see who I am and would admire me.'
'Poor ego!' replied my soul. 'Not only do you live in hypoc-

[45]. Adapted from Shi Bhagavan Aryadeva, *The Words of the Guru*, Lotus/Chou, 1980.

risy and slander, but you want to die in them.'
Then this Sufi vowed never to leave his cave:
'What other victory would I seek but victory over my own desires, including trying to change the world or convert it? Trying to change myself is the only true battle. And it does no harm to anyone.'[46]

*'The only holy war is the war against oneself, nobody else,' said Sheikh Assam echoing the Buddha: 'Even though one may conquer a thousand men in the battlefield a thousand times, the one, who conquers himself is the noblest victor.*[47]

---

[46]. Adapted from Rumi : *In the Arms of the Beloved*, translation John Star, The Putnam Publishing Group,1997.
[47]. Cheikh Assam in Patrick. Levy, *Dieu croit-il en Dieu ?*, Albin Michel/ Question de, 1993. Then Buddha, Dhammapada, 103.

## One or many? It's Devotion that counts

Monotheism has always been presented as an undisputable measure of humanity's progress. Believing in only one God was supposed to be better than worshipping several.

The monotheists, who are in favour of this belief, have no real proof of the existence of this one God. They have no more proof of this than those believing in the reality of many Gods have of the reality of theirs. Like them, they only believe something, but the truth is they don't know.

However, though this preference is not sure, it bears dangerous consequences. If I believe there is only one God, then I must also believe that the one I believe in is the true one. I also have to believe that the One-and-only-God, which is different from mine, or the many Gods which others believe in, are not the true ones. But if those believing in a different One-and-only-God, or in many Gods, are happy and prosperous, their mere existence poses a threat to my own faith. They believe in what I see as untrue Gods, yet nothing more catastrophic happens to them than what I experience. Their God or Gods are no more and no less benevolent than my one; they don't protect them any more or less than mine protects me. In fact they show me that it doesn't really matter.

For a few people this is so unbearable that it triggers violence. They cannot cope with the evidence of the relativity of their beliefs. For them, everybody must believe in what they believe in for the world to be orderly and intelligible. So they try to make themselves the ones who are responsible for producing this order. Why don't they let God take care of his own problems?

Hindus believe that God has many forms, many names and many stories… They worship rivers, trees, idols, animal-Gods, Gods with eight arms, various One-and-only-Gods, avatars, the Moon, the Sun, Time... and some try to experience the direct knowledge of non-duality, or the unity of the perceiver and perceived. Every conceivable demonstration of the sacred from time immemorial endures with them. They deem that preferring a particular God is simply a matter of affinity.

For Hindus, devotion itself is what really counts, not to whom the devotion is addressed. Devotion is the attitude by which the ego takes pleasure in diminishing. It is not a question of believing, it is more about loving and blessing.

They are not afraid of making images of Gods. They are not afraid of saying that God is also beyond the images, and that there is something beyond God as well: the Brahman, the unique impersonal consciousness.

The Hindus' polytheist option poses no threat to anyone's belief for, if there are many Gods, one that anyone believes in might also be fine.

Mankind as a whole is polytheist, for some people believe in a One-and-only-God, some in a different One-and-only-God, some in one with exceptions, some in many, some in none…

The Hindu alternative is the most tolerant, the closest to humanity's real situation, and the one which is in harmony with everybody's own affinities.

*'Don't tell me what you believe in, tell me how you know', Rabbi Rachi used to say.*

## In everything

Narendra's guru once asked :
'House holders speak ill of those who dedicate themselves to God. When an elephant walks along a road, dogs run around him barking, but he goes on as if he didn't hear them. Imagine people were to speak ill of you behind your back, what would you think?'
'I would consider them as small dogs barking behind me,' Narendra answered.
'No, Shree Ramakrishna replied laughingly, you're not an elephant. You know that God dwells in all things. Therefore all things must become objects of worship: people, animals, plants and minerals.'[48]

[48]. *The Gospel of Sri Râmakrishna*, swami Nikkhilananda ; Râmakrishna-Vivekananda Center; New-York; 1942.

# The Four Noble Truths

*Does God exist? Does he not exist? It doesn't matter! The Buddha's response was that it is important is to overcome every kind of suffering and to know what they consist of. This, perhaps, is wisdom.*

In his first sermon Buddha announced four correct, just, pure, unalterable, noble truths. The truth of dukkha, the cause of dukkha, the cessation of dukkha and the path leading to the cessation of dukkha. What is *dukkha*? Suffering and misery of suffering, misfortune, pain, dissatisfaction.

For several years before his enlightenment, Shakyamuni, who later became the Buddha, lived with five ascetics, and practiced severe austerities and mortifications with them. One day, he understood that these practices would lead him nowhere and he gave them up. His five, disgruntled companions subsequently abandoned him.

Sometime later, Shakyamuni reached enlightenment by other methods. He found his former companions in the Deer Park near Varanasi and explained his Middle Way: neither exaggerated asceticism nor self-indulgence. It was a path of moderation between the extremes of self-mortification and gratifying one's every desire and leading a slack life. 'In this very one-fathom-long body, along with its perceptions and thoughts, do I proclaim the world, the origin of the world, the cessation of the world, and the path leading to the cessation of the world', he said. 'I expect nothing from God, for liberation is within oneself.' He based his doctrine on four principles

known as The Four Noble Truths.
'Birth is suffering, aging is suffering, illness is suffering, death is suffering; sorrow, lamentation, pain, grief and despair are suffering; union with what is displeasing is suffering; separation from what is pleasing is suffering; not getting what one wants is suffering; in short, the five aggregates subject to clinging are suffering.
The origin of suffering is this craving which leads to the renewal of existence and becoming. It is accompanied by delight and lust, seeking delight here and there, that is, craving for sensual pleasures, craving for existence and craving for non-existence.
This is the noble truth of the cessation of suffering: it is the complete extinction and cessation of that same craving, the giving up and relinquishing of it, freedom from it, non-reliance on it.'
The Path leading to the cessation of suffering is the Noble Eightfold Path; that is: right view, right intention, right speech, right action, right livelihood, right effort, right mindfulness and right concentration.'
Right view means to grasp the impermanent and imperfect nature of worldly objects and ideas.
Right intention means being mentally in agreement with right view.
Right speech means to tell the truth, to speak in a friendly, warm, and gentle manner and only to talk when necessary.
Right action means to act kindly and compassionately, to be honest, to respect the belongings of others, and to maintain sexual relationships which do not harm others. So it also means

to abstain from harming or killing sentient beings, to abstain from taking what is not given.

Right livelihood means that one should earn one's living in a way that does not harm other beings: dealing in weapons, dealing in living beings, working in meat production and butchery, and selling intoxicants and poisons.

Right effort means turning energy that fuels desire, envy, aggression, and violence into self-discipline, honesty, benevolence, and kindness.

Right mindfulness is the mental ability to see and to understand things as they really are, with clear consciousness.

Right concentration, refers to the development of a mental strength described as one-pointedness of mind, meaning a state where all mental faculties are unified and directed onto one particular object.[49]

*'Everything which has the nature of appearance, also has the nature of cessation,' is what the Buddha teaches. So it is in desire that we find ways to overcome desires. The attachment contains the root of detachment. The world and ourselves are united in this connection which is found within ourselves. Therefore transformation begins within ourselves.*

---

[49]. Dhamma-Cakkappavattana-Sutta; The Four Noble Truths. And Anguttara-nikâya.

# The dreadful thief

*'Purity is not a prerequisite for grace. Grace does not come because of one's merits. The worst sinners have received it and become pure and glorious. Those who receive grace don't ever think they deserved it,'*

*- Ramdas.*

A long time ago, in India, there lived a terrible thief. Even today he is considered to be the most dreadful bandit of all time. He was swift and clever, courageous and ruthless. When he was seen in Varanasi, he was also reported to be in Jaipur or Islamabad! Everybody feared him as though he were a demon.

One day God appeared to him in the form of Lord Shiva and said:

'You are the greatest bandit of all time, so why did you never think of stealing me?'

God is indeed the greatest of the great thieves, for he takes souls into divine rapture.

The bandit then resolved to quit. 'I am no demon, I'm a human being. I will give up my old ways and never return to them.' He then became the most ardent devotee of Lord Shiva.

Ananda Giri Ma added to this legend by saying: 'Nothing is ever fixed, set, final, forever. You can always be seized by the divine. To be taken by him, you don't have to go very far, just get very deep inside yourself, right to the bottom, where you haven't looked yet. There is no devil here. If you stick to clichés or preconceived ideas concerning the divine, you are still far from the light, in murky waters. It is very close, very close. We are whole and complete. Go deeper and deeper down within yourself, and at some point you'll know that it's there. You'll see it for sure if you get there. That is where he seizes you.'[50]

*There is no saint without a past, and no sinner without a future, said Haidakhandi Babaji.*

---

[50]. Ananda Giri Maï, in Patrick. Levy, *Dieu leur parle-t-Il ?* Desclée de Brouwer, 1997. This bandit is supposed to be Vâlmîkî, the author of the Râmâyana.

# Who is in charge?

Ever since the beginning of the world, God could see, looking down from heaven, that his Creation was not doing well. In a moment volcanoes and earthquakes could eliminate what life had created over thousands of years; tidal waves swallowed living beings by the thousands; storms and hurricanes destroyed crops and shelters; diseases swarmed and decimated entire populations; animals devoured each other. Disasters and suffering affected all living beings. And men added further ordeals to their suffering by killing each other.

What can I do? God asked himself. What can I do?

Then he had an idea.

From heaven above, God started to pray. He prayed to the volcanoes, to the seas and oceans, clouds and diseases, to the animals and men...

After one or two thousand years, God saw that his prayers had had no effect in preventing continents from drifting and causing devastating earthquakes, hurricanes from destroying, rivers from flooding, diseases from proliferating, animals from devouring each other, and men from killing one another. Everything and everyone was heading towards an unknown destiny, and it seemed that nothing could do much to change it.

Worst of all, those to whom God was praying, were in fact praying to him! Some men beseeched him, some glorified him. They were praying so hard that they were deaf to his prayers.

So, after God had prayed for some time, and having realized that no one was listening to his prayers, he destroyed all of humanity and every other living being in a flood which cov-

ered the entire earth, causing more pain in one day than all of the ills of the earth in centuries. A few men, their families and some animals managed to escape the disaster and went on to repopulate the world. However nothing had really changed.
So God came to the understanding that he just had to let it be. Once he had resigned himself to this, he leaned over to examine the Earth one last time, and then he had another idea: 'I'll inspire human beings to have wisdom and doubt. Then every time they have hardships it will remind them that I am powerless. And they'll understand that they are responsible for the good and evil that they create, even though they are innocent of the hardships that befall them.
But very few men received the gift of wisdom. Most refused to understand that God was powerless and that the main objective was to avoid adding suffering to suffering. They proclaimed religions which stated that ordeals were God's punishments. They also declared the things that God wanted, what he had ordered, what he would do if people did otherwise, how he would punish those who did not obey, and how the pious ones would punish those who did not believe in these things.
People were attempting to escape the insecurities and precariousness of life through wild dreams that were even more frightening.
So they began to convert people or kill them in the name of whatever name they gave God!
Centuries passed like this.
God withdrew far from this world and its restlessness. He vowed never to appear to anyone, anywhere, ever again.
'Maybe one day they will stop praying to me and start praying to each other!'

# Studying

*Judaism is not something that is taught. It's the practice of questioning through studying texts. Studying means practicing questioning. This opens routes of inquiry which, in turn, open out infinitely into new ones. Therefore, the infinite is contained in study yet it is not limited by it in any way.*

*'God gave us the Holy Book,' the rabbis reason, 'therefore it no longer belongs to him.' This means that everyone is allowed to read it, study it, understand it, debate with it, try to make out what it does say from what it doesn't say. 'Elohim spoke once, but twice I heard,' declared David. The second time is studying. 'Look!' said Rabbi Simeon: 'Darkness, is the black ink of the Holy Book (the written words) but light is in the white spaces of the page (what is between the letters). Study again.*

'Isn't God within man? the disciple asked Rabbi Isaac.

'God is inside or outside, but also inside and outside, and yet neither inside nor outside. So where is he?'

As his disciple was not answering, the rabbi added:

'It's a mystery game!'

The disciple was silent, the rabbi exclaimed:

'God is in the mystery game itself! He dwells in the heart of the questions we ask, in that which we don't know, and not in our answers.'

Rabbi Isaac took the Talmud out of his bookshelves, opened it and said:

'Well, look at this mystery. The Treaty Haguiga focuses on the verse: "Question the days from the day God created man on earth'. Why is it written "from the day?" Why should we only question from "when God created man on earth?" So we have this extraordinary comment: "The one who seeks to unravel the mystery of what is above, below, before and after, it would have been better for him to have never been created."

That which is forbidden always also indicates that which is allowed and is therefore used to point out where to look, but it is the seeker's own responsibility to find his own way to an answer which will also be a question. If it is forbidden to question that which is "above, below, before and after," then questioning and seeking in between is allowed. What else is there?'

The disciple drew a little sketch. He drew a point, another below, a point on the right between the first two and a fourth on the left.

'Between above, below, before and after... what is there?' he asked.

'It's up to you to tell me.'

'I am trying...'

'Very good! You have already found that what's important is to search! What's in the centre?' the rabbi asked.

In centre, the disciple drew a question mark.

'The centre is a question mark,' he said.

The rabbi smiled.

'Exactly. You could also have placed "me" in the centre... or "I", or God, or here and now, or the Holy Book, or even a pink elephant, or you could have left a void… as long as it makes you reflect on man or God.

That which creates man and makes him surpass himself to reach beyond the human condition, are his questions. They connect him both to his most distant ancestors and to infinity. The answers we risk making, and which sometimes give rise to religions, are completely insignificant in the light of the unutterable.

Don't search above, below, before or after yourself, look within yourself. Once there, look for questions, your own questions rather than answers. And when you think you have found an answer, remember that there are no fewer than seventy for any one question. Seventy answers, that means that searching is infinite. Searching is the infinite itself.'

And he concluded:

'If all the answers were known, we would be their prisoners; and we would remain under their domination. The mystery of life, its need for meaning and God's elusiveness all give us freedom. So this freedom that can be found by observing mysteries, can be practiced through studying and questioning...'[51]

[51]. Rabbi Isaac Goldman, in *Le Kabbaliste*, Patrick. Levy, Pocket 2003. Deuteronomi 4:32.

## To be or not to be

Two Talmudic schools fought for two and a half years over the question: 'Would it be better to have not been born? Or is it a blessing for living beings to be alive?'

Then, after two and a half years of debate, they voted. The school of Rabbi Chammaï won. The tradition mentions this commentary: 'It would have been better if man had not been born, but since he was born, he should carry out a self-examination, question the meaning of his actions, seek in himself the right path to take.'

'In order to answer a basic existential question: "why is there life?' Or "Is it better not to be born?' the rabbis force everyone to look into themselves,' commented Rabbi Isaac.

'Questioning the meaning of one's own actions is an attempt to observe the motivations behind them, or even the singular underlying motivation. By searching within oneself, the root of any act; seeing the desire, and then below, the drive which triggered its idea, its need or its necessity; a personal and universal answer is revealed in this introspection: I want to live. The root of any of my actions, regardless of the act, always reveals this. Whatever forms they take, it is always the desire to be and the desire to live which act in me.

Seeing this and understanding that you are responsible, as the guardian and even the creator of your own life impulse, that you approve of your existence, is a path you can take, a possible means to progress spiritually.

Perhaps God created life, but was he aware that if humans had to live they would end up liking life and that they would

lose themselves by creating new desires?
So, the story that's being written looks like a love story: the infinite and the finite, the creator and the creature, the absolute and the relative are looking for each other, but they take countless detours to reach each other. God, the Eternal in the heart of man, waits in love while man loses his way in the pursuit of desires. One day, man realizes that love is the foundation rather than a relationship: it's not loving something, but that everything is love. Then, desire and love meet, and God reveals himself in that encounter.
This is the meaning of the God's fearing: seeing the blessedness and fragile beauty which we call fear… the fear of parting with them even for a single moment. A state of grace.
It would have been better if man had not been born, but since he was born, he should search the meaning of what it is to be, not be, desire and love.'[52]

*'The desire to have a soul and be immortal only within this soul, must be particularly pale when compared to the desire of a soul to have a body, and a duration. It would give up its kingdom for that.'*[53]

---

52. The talmudic question : Talmud de Babylone, Haguiga 11b.
53. By Paul Valéry, *Tel Quel*, Gallimard; 1941

## What does a man have that God does not?

*For Carl Gustav Jung, if God is omnipotent, he has no means of being conscious of anything, not even himself. For consciousness arises from confrontation. 'By virtue of his omnipotence, God never encounters an insurmountable obstacle that is likely to make him hesitate and thus reflect upon himself...'*[54]

A man was reflecting about God: 'Why did the Almighty feel the desire, and may be the need, to create something? Is it possible for a limitless, all-including, omnipotent, omniscient being to have a need? If he had a desire, we would have to assume that something was missing! How could that which includes the whole be missing something? How can this Creation, and man in it, be of any use of to a God who is already everything? What purpose would they fulfil?'

Our man was thinking like this. His questions inevitably led him to conclude that man's conceptions of God were either absurd, childish or naive. But he could not find any other.

One day, upon resuming his reflections, he inverted the problem. 'In order to increase God's prestige, man devalues himself and does not recognize his own qualities. Man may be better than God! If man means something to God, then his creation is justified.' So, he asked himself a new question: 'What does a man have that God does not?'

---

[54]. C.G.Jung, *Answer to Job.*

Our man meditated on it for some time. He thought: 'Man has a body. God does not have one. Man is limited, God is infinite. But his body, through its aptitudes, qualities, functions and limitations, gives man the ability to taste, feel and enjoy Creation. Having dealings with that which is not him, he confronts obstacles that awaken in him a certain capacity for self-reflection. He can find qualities to his experiences: pleasant or unpleasant, good or bad, sweet or bitter, and the development of the subtlety of his subjectivity is infinite.
Without a body, the Creator has no means of knowing Creation. But through Man who is part of himself he has access to the five senses to feel, his intellect to understand and give meaning, and a 'spiritual breath' to know God. Thus, through man, God can know His creation, and know himself.
In the image of God, man also reflects God,' he concluded.

*'I was a hidden treasure that wished to be known, so I created Creation so that I could know it (or know myself...)' (Hadith Qudsi. 19) The hidden meanings of each word of this hadith are a treasure in themselves.*[55]

[55]. Hadith are words attributed to God in the Muslim tradition.

# The divine is an 'us'

We once asked Ananda Giri Ma of Aveyron:
'What are you talking about when you talk about "God"?'
'The divine is an "us", it is "us",' she said. In Sanskrit, Aham is the supreme "I", the transcendental "I", an "I" which includes everything in an indivisible unity and in which everything forms an "us". The ego, ahamkara, is an "I" who acts, produces causes and effects, and creates a smaller "I", a "not-us". The ego creates a separate "I". It constructs this separation.
Ma, in Sanskrit, means mother, the origin of everything. The universe is Ma. And Ma also means the measure. The measure is the universe. Mâyâ, the illusion, the miscomprehension, is to lose the measure. The real individual is the universe itself, anyone who measures himself as an individual smaller than the universe is in the illusion of a separation. He has lost the measure, his origin. The opening is to understand that this separation is illusory. From this perspective, anything is possible.
This divine is in you, in your own openness to everything, no more and no less. If this is your attitude, then irresistibly you are him and he is you. And then the whole world bears the message of what is to be loved in everything, whatever there is. There are no exceptions; everything carries this message, if you can accept to see it. Within love there is no other possibility. Everything becomes a message… of the Beloved.
There is nothing else to do but to complete the movement of things from one moment to another. To complete it is to add whatever you can give it. Whatever it is, you will know. The

calmer you are, the clearer it will be what you can do. Don't try to predict. Let peace come to you. Let it enter you without you filling it with something.'[56]

*'Can you walk on water? If so you're no better than a straw. Can you fly in the air? If so you're no better than a fly. Only when you are the master of your heart can you truly become somebody.' - Ansari of Herat.*

[56]. Ananda Giri Maï, in Patrick. Levy, *Dieu leur parle-t-Il ?*, Desclée de Brouwer, 1997.

## Show me God

Once when Swami Rama was a young disciple, one morning, he rushed over to his guru demanding:
'I want to see God! Show me God!'
'Okay, okay!' his guru replied calmly. 'I'll show you God tomorrow.'
Swami Rama went back the next day.
'You promised to show me God.'
'Tell me first, which God do you want to see? What kind of God are you willing to meet?'
'Are there so many kinds of gods?'
'Everybody wants to see God. But first, you must think about it intensely and have a firm belief in your mind and heart about God. How do you define God? How do you conceptualize him? If you're looking for God without being sure about what you are looking for, what will you find? If I tell you that everything you see is God, you will answer 'No, this or that is not God'. If I tell you that God is in you, you will not be satisfied because right now you don't see it like that. And if God appeared here as a sign or in the form of an animal or a man, you would, all the same, still have doubts. Tell me what you expect God to be and I'll show you that God. I will show you God exactly according to your definition and conviction.'
'I'll think about it,' said Swami Rama.
'But beware!' added his guru, 'God is beyond our mental faculties. He appears in the intuition of truth. Go and meditate and when you're ready, come back and see me.'
Swami Rama then tells us: 'So I tried to imagine what God

might look like, but my imagination would not go further than a form, be it animal, human or cosmic. I often had the mental picture of an old wise, powerful and benevolent man, and soon I realized how naïve my request was. Finally, I went back to my guru and said:

'Show me the God who can free us from misery and bring us happiness.'

'This is a state of peace and equipoise that everyone must achieve by himself! Haven't I already shown you how?

'Then show me the God that the saints see when they call him.'

'Okay, listen to this story, through it God will appear to you:

Malidas was a cowherd who lived near Varanasi. In the morning he would take his cattle to the pasture through the track which runs alongside Ganges, and in the evening, he brought them back. He was illiterate, innocent and a bit simple.

One day, he paid more attention to Swami Prakash, a Brahmin, who performed his ablutions on the banks of the Ganges. The Swami sat on the shore, said prayers and practiced pranayama (a breath control practice which enables one to have control over the body's energy flows.). As he was about to go, Malidas bowed at his feet and asked him for initiation:

"You're illiterate, you wouldn't understand! Let me go," replied Swami Prakash.

"Okay, but at least answer this question: Why did you hold your nose?"

"By holding our nose and stopping our breath, our mind can concentrate more easily. Through concentration we can see

God!"
Malidas let Swami Prakash go. But from then on, he regarded him as his guru. He took a bath in the river and then sat on the shore and stopped breathing whilst holding his nose. After a minute he began to worry: "God has not come yet; maybe he is busy?" However, he continued holding his breath and his nose, but a minute later God had still not appeared and Malidas was beginning to choke. Yet he still remained firm. One more minute and Malidas would faint... At this very moment Vishnu appeared to Malidas. He had four arms, was dressed in silk brocade and hallowed by a disk of light.
"I am God," said Vishnu. "You called me?"
"How can I be sure that you are God?" replied Malidas. "I must call my guru. If he says that you are God, I'll be satisfied."
"Very well, call him."
"But you may be gone when I come back!"
"No, I'll stay here," promised Vishnu.
"But how can I believe you?"
Malidas took a rope from one of his cows' neck and tied Vishnu to a tree. Then he ran in search of Swami Prakash. He soon found him, and in spite of his reluctances, he compelled him to follow him. Of course, Swami Prakash saw nothing, but to get rid of his troublesome disciple he agreed that Vishnu was indeed there before them, and he left.
Then, Vishnu granted Malidas a wish.
"When I stop breathing and hold my nose, you will appear immediately. You will not be late, like today." This was Malida's wish.
Vishnu agreed.

Time passed and sometime later Malidas had acquired the reputation of a saint. At times he would call on Vishnu and Vishnu appeared to him.

One day, Swami Prakash came back that way, on the shore of Ganga. Malidas rushed to his feet and bowed again and again and thanked him for having shown him the right way to see God. As the Brahmin could not understand, Malidas told him that since they last met, when he wanted to see Vishnu, he just stopped breathing whilst holding his nose, and Vishnu appeared promptly. Swami Prakash realized that his disciple was much closer to God than he had ever been whilst performing every prescribed rituals and being obsessed by his cast purity. He prostrated himself before the feet of his disciple and asked for instructions to purify his heart and see God.

Malidas ordered him to become a cowherd and to pray constantly for a whole year.

"In one year, if you have overcome your anger, your pride and your selfishness, come to see me after taking a bath.

One year later, Malidas told his neighbour to throw some dust on Swami Prakash once he'd taken his bath.

The man did as requested and Prakash became mad with rage. He ran after the man to beat him, the took a bath once again and went to see Malidas:

"A year has passed, Guruji. Now, can I see God?"

"Your heart is not pure. Anger can take hold of it at any time. Take care of your cows and pray constantly for another year," Malidas ordered him. Swami Prakash obeyed.

The day the second year ended, Malidas told his neighbour

to throw some dust on Swami Prakash after his bath. This time, the Brahmin didn't run after him, however he abused him vehemently, then took a second bath and went to see Malidas.

"Your heart is not pure yet. Anger, just like a snake, still dwells in it, ready to pounce. Practice for another year."

The Brahmin obeyed. The day the third year ended, Malidas told his neighbour to throw dust on Prakash after he'd taken his bath. This time Prakash understood that this man was a manifestation of God to help him overcome anger. He prostrated himself at his feet and thanked him, then he went to his guru.

"Now you see God," said Malidas. "You do not need me."

And Swami Rama realized that one cannot ask someone else to show him God.

In his state of ignorance and naivety, the disciple believes that God is a particular being with special qualities like might and benevolence, or that he is the force that manifests the universe, the fountain of Love, the absolute Reality, the real Self of all things... but when he realizes that the God he longs for and wishes to meet is necessarily within oneself, buried somewhere in his belief, then he knows that no one can show it to someone else.[57]

[57]. The first story is inspired by an idea of Swami Rama, *Living with the Himalayan Masters*, International Institute of Yoga Science, 1978. The second story is Freely adapted from a tale told by Swami Sivananda, *Inspiring Stories*, Divine Life Society Publication, Sivanandanagar, UP, 1997.

# Tao

There was something
formless and perfect
Before Heaven-and-Earth were born.
It is serene. Empty.
Causeless. Unchanging.
Infinite. Eternally present.
It may be the mother of the universe.
Not knowing its name, I call it Tao.
For lack of a better word, I call it great.

Look, and it can't be seen.
Listen, and it can't be heard.
Reach, and it can't be grasped.
These three qualities whose essence is incomprehensible blend into Unity.

Above, it isn't bright. Below, it isn't dark.
Seamless, unnameable, it returns to the realm of nothing.
Form of the formless,
Imageless image,
subtle, beyond conception.
Approaching it you don't see where it begins;
following it you don't see where it ends.[58]

[58]. Lao Tseu, *Tao Tô Kin*; XXV et XIV.

## Unity

He was one with the One. He was one with all beings, as if connected to the heart of everything by a silk thread. When he contemplated, sitting on a rock, lichen ate away at his robe. When he contemplated sitting on a flower, bees pollinated his hair. When he was meditating sitting on the sea, cormorants went fishing in his sleeves.

He was called to the temple. The priest questioned him, putting an egg in front of him.

He took the egg and placed it on the tip of the jade needle of his bun.

Nobody asked him how and why he did this. But sometimes, those who hear this story dream of becoming like him.[59]

*'Talk about philosophy as much as you can, worship as many gods as you please, sing songs of praises devotedly to any number of divine beings, liberation will never happen, even after one hundred centuries, if you do not have awareness of the Unicity of the Self', said Shankarachaya.*

[59]. M.F.Turpaud, *Le Tarot de Marseille*, Solar, 1987.

## Jnaneshvari

The Self is neither divided nor whole, neither active nor inactive, neither slender nor gross, for it is without attributes;
It is neither visible nor invisible, neither perceptible nor imperceptible, neither shining nor dark, neither small nor large, because it has no form;
It is neither empty nor full, neither with nor without possessions, neither with nor without form, for it is the void.
It does not feel joy and is not enlightened either; it is neither one nor many, neither free nor bound. That's what the Self is.

Just like the fruit is in flower, the flower in the bud, the bud in the branch, the branch in the tree, the tree in the seed and the seed in the fruit, in the same way 'I am" is everywhere, and there is nothing outside of the universal Self.
Flame and fire are one; the lotus petals are joined to the flower, and the fruit and the branch are the tree itself, in the same way the entire universe is the Self.
Moisture is in water, space in the sky, sweetness in sugar: between them, there is no real separation.
When this vision of the unity is awakened, one finds the vessel of divine wealth on which one can cross the ocean of life.
Then, wherever one looks, he only sees the divine and enters infinite bliss.

The Self neither takes nor leaves the body. Even if it exists in the body, the body does not alter it.
It doesn't act, nor does it cause action. It doesn't even pro-

duce the slightest fortuitous event. It is eternally the same. Thus, it is dependent on neither more nor less.
Just like sparks of fire, all created forms are rooted in the One.
When the clay pot is broken and its pieces are thrown away, the air it contained mixes with the surrounding air everywhere. Similarly, when the perception 'I am this body' dies with the body, if a man remembers his true nature, he reaches unity and nothing else. He immediately becomes one with the Self.
When the wind of concern with the body ceases to blow, O warrior! the individual soul attains union with the divine just like waves merge into the ocean.
Although you still remain in your body, you are dependent no more on its birth titles and attributes.

Just like the waves of the ocean, the sun's rays, the atoms of the earth, and the limbs of the body, the body sensations arise in the mind.
Like a fish in the waters of earthly existence, you have to experience pleasure and pain, nevertheless disregard them both through being established in your true nature.
As the seed is separated from husks, as the river Ganges, having run its course, joins with the ocean and leaves behind its turbulent flow
Similarly, O conqueror of the ultimate wealth, pleasures and pains are equally accepted as the conditions of bodily life by the one who has begun to dwell in the Self.

Just like the largest wave is no different from the ocean, there

is not any difference between you and the universal Self. Just as gold is one with the ornament fashioned from it, and a ray is emitted by light, yet the ray is also the light itself, so you should realize that you are in me.
Don't consider yourself different from the Self. You are part of self like an atom of dust is part of the earth.
When one's outlook is illuminated by the experience of oneness, we call this devotion.

There is but only one thread woven throughout a fabric, in the same way acknowledge only the Self in the entire universe.
Just as the water falls effortlessly, let it be your nature to give equal respect to all creatures.
As the fruit laden branch naturally bends down towards the ground, bow before all creatures.
Without being concerned with one's own greatness, the conqueror of ultimate truth does not distinguish between what has valuc and what docs not. Putting cverything ncatly together, he bows down with delight to everything.[60]

[60]. Jnaneshvari, from chapters 9, 13 et 14.

## Just don't think about it

*'Do not build your understanding and your beliefs on your senses and your thoughts," said the sage Huang Po, 'but at the same time, don't seek a mind which is distinct from your senses and your thoughts: don't try to grasp reality through rejecting your senses and your thoughts. When you are neither attached to them, nor detached from them, then you enjoy freedom. Unimpeded in this way they are your foundations for enlightenment.'*

That day, before zazen, the teacher told a story…
A basket maker lived in an old house in the mountains. He was working near the fire when the Old-girl-of-the-mountain arrived:
'It's freezing cold!' she said in her hoarse voice.
The basket maker thought: 'What bad luck; the fierce Old-girl-of-the-mountain is here. I'll have to throw ashes at her or she'll eat me...'
The old woman whispered: 'Ha ha! you want to throw ashes at me…'
Taken aback, the basket maker thought: 'I shall cut her into pieces.'
She asked:
'Ha ha! you want to cut me into pieces?'
The basket-maker understood that the Old woman was guessing his thoughts and that she would soon take hold of him. Then she confirmed it once again:

'Ha ha! You're scared, eh?'
He decided to stop thinking about her and continued his work, focusing on intertwining each stalk of cane.
Raising his head to put down his finished basket and start a new one he saw that the Old woman was gone. In her place, there was a small heap of cold ashes…'
At the end of zazen, a man got up, apparently distressed, and he whispered to his neighbour:
'I can't stop thinking.'
'Well, don't think about it!' he replied.[61]

*'Everything that appears in the mind and disappears in mind is but the mind itself'. Patanjali.*

[61]. « *The Old-Girl-of-the-Montain* », freely adapted from a Japanese tale : *History of Buddhism*, Keisai, 1976, Tokyo. Then the distressed zazen practitioner : Jacques Brosse, *Zen et Occident*, Albin Michel, 1992.

## The spiritual experience

*Abbot Pierre was talking about days past when he would spend his time carrying furniture for the newly formed Emmaus Companions: 'At night,' he said, 'I was broken, tired and exhausted, but thinking of the work we'd accomplished I felt joy. This joy is God.'*

*Andre Frossard recounts his encounters with the divine: 'I'm not saying the sky opens, it doesn't open, it leaps forward, it ascends suddenly, a silent fulguration, in this improbable chapel in which it is mysteriously included...'*

*'It's like a passage to death. It so happens that the pulse is almost gone,' Saint Teresa of Avila wrote. 'Often my body seems so light that I don't feel its weight, and to such an extent that at times I just don't know if my feet are touching the ground.'*

*'And everything is strange and new...' wrote Robert Browning.*

'What are we looking for? What do we look for when we look for God?' The Pir intensely asked his disciples to consider.

If we have a precise idea of what God is, he will remain unknown and unknowable. We don't know how God will appear to us, in what form he will manifest, and most of all if we will recognize him... God does not necessarily reveal himself the way we expect.

But from time to time, we all experience an intuition of sorts, a moment of harmony, a special feeling, full of meaning, a lightness, an enlightenment, a sense of communion with everything and everyone which gives us the sense of a unified, coherent and beneficial reality. It may be a moment of peace, serenity or joy.

We all have known such moments though we would describe them in our own ways. We don't always recognize them for what they are. We don't recognize their value because we do not know what we are looking for in the spiritual adventure. Thus, we let them fade away. Yet, these are possibly mystical experiences.

Be aware of moments when the borderline between outer and inner disappears, when time seems suspended, the sudden sensation of unreality, or a feeling of closeness with everything around you.

Even though it is significant, this experience is not permanent. It does not transform us suddenly and forever. It comes and goes. However that doesn't make it unimportant.

It happens spontaneously, but we can also work at it through the different means taught by spiritual and philosophical traditions.

Be aware of these moments in which the infinite calls upon you.

*'All of our mental and physical explorations are carried out within ourselves, as though they were in a vase. This vase is our physical and spiritual individuality. We can never get out of ourselves. There is no escape outside of oneself, nor out of the world in which we live. For this world is not outside ourselves, but inside' - Alexandra David-Neel.*

# SatCitAnanda Brahman

*The Hindu's advaïta (non-duality) philosophy promises that 'knowledge more than action (karma) destroys ignorance'. It pledges: 'learning and studying the principles of advaïta makes it possible to understand and to have an indirect knowledge of the One-without-a-Second. However this indirect knowledge can be instantly transformed into direct knowledge.' Until then, 'reasoning drives out the traces of darkness and confusion, reflection illuminates, and meditation is the direct realization of Brahman as consciousness in its own form.' The Rig Veda, the Upanishads, the vedanta and treaties of the Masters of advaïta like Sankaracharia, swami Vidyaranya and Narayana Guru model this darshan, this point of view.*

Swami Anandababa taught it in various ways:
'The absolute *Brahman* can be known through *sat*, *cit* or *ananda*, (*sat*: being, existence and reality; *cit*: intelligence-consciousness itself; *ananda*: bliss, the underlying all-pervading bliss).
This is called looking for the nature of *Brahman* through the path of consciousness (*cit*): The first modification of the One-without-a-Second is *Prakriti*. *Prakriti* is the "second", the first effect of differentiation. It is the second moment which creates movement. It starts with emptiness. Emptiness before space. Emptiness without space,' insisted my guru as if he wanted to empty it even more. 'When one takes the idea of space away from emptiness, what remains?'
'Nothing,' I asserted with confidence.
'That which is represented by the concept *nothing* is thus revealed to consciousness (*cit*). Existence (*sat*) should therefore be allotted to it. Producing no misery, it is also bliss (*ananda*).

Consequently there remains not *nothing* but *SatCitAnanda* (existence, consciousness, and bliss). The common element to everything represented by names and forms is *SatCitAnanda*. This is a direct knowledge of *SatCitAnanda Brahman*. Your mind, thinking of emptiness which cannot contain anything (without space) is emptied of anything else, and thus reveals nothingness to itself, and makes the reflection of consciousness in its immutable nature occur.

While you seek this emptiness without space, your consciousness observes nothingness, sees the existence of *nothing* and thus can observe itself in it. And this is beyond suffering.

See that.'

(...)

'When a pot is broken, clay is still there. When the body is burned, ashes remain. There is *nothing* left when names and forms disappear, but this *nothing* is still consciousness knowing the destruction of names and forms.

There is no outside of consciousness. Through its energy the universe is known. Through its light it appears in every act of knowing. Consciousness is knowledge. Without knowledge, you cannot even say that you don't know. Consciousness is neither the known nor the unknown. It knows everything that is knowable: the object and subject.

The presence or the absence of something is knowledge. It cannot be anything else but knowledge, whether there is or is not anything behind this knowledge.

See that.'

(...)

'Take this jar full of water. Look in it. Water occupies all the space within the jar, therefore the space in the jar is contained in the water.'

'Yes,' I answered trustfully.
'Now, look at the surface of the water, the reflection of the moon and the stars. That outer space is also contained in the water. The water in the jar and space in the sky are both contained in the space limited by the jar. It is only a play of illusion. In the same way, the one Self is in the body and in everything else.
This is a *darshan*, the direct knowledge, of *Brahman* as *atman* (self). The space delimited by the jar is hidden by the water which it contains and by the sky which it reflects, in just the same way as the unchanging reality (*Brahman*) is hidden by vitality (*atman as jiva, an individual self*).
See that.'
(...)
'In deep sleep, the mind is absorbed in its cause, undifferentiated ignorance, and everything is calm. During *samadhi*, consciousness is focused on the *atman* (self) as an object, and is subjected to no subjective knowledge from manas (the mental function). In deep sleep and *samadhi*, free from mental activity, *jiva* (personal consciousness) has direct knowledge of the *ananda* (bliss) of *SatCitAnanda Brahman*.'
'Can we call "knowledge" deep sleep even though consciousness is absent?' I objected.
'Everyone knows what deep sleep is, although consciousness is absent. One has a positive memory of it. Memory presupposes experience. We love deep sleep. When we wake up, we still feel how nice it was! We remember it as bliss. Just as happiness and sorrow are knowledge, their absence is knowledge as well.
In deep sleep, a blind man is not blind; a wounded man is not hurt. Consciousness has an immediate experience of knowing the absence of grief. And as grief is the opposite of bliss, its

absence is bliss.'

'If, when I feel *nothing*, neither pain nor pleasure, that is bliss, this stone must also be in bliss,' I still objected.

'Objects know neither sorrow nor joy. They do not know their absence,' refuted my guru. 'When the knower disappears, bliss is revealed. The Self is known by the Self.

See that'

(...)

'Here is a way to find the nature of *Brahman* through the path of existence (*sat*):

The existence of space, distinct from the *Brahman*, is possible because of its properties in the realm of name and form. The properties of space are to give volume, to allow movement and in some cases carry sound. Space exists in its properties; it is its dharma.

But in space, as in all things, it is being or existence (*sat*) which appears first and foremost. If you remove existence from space, space disappears. But if we remove space from existence, existence remains.

This is a direct knowledge of *sat-Brahman*.

The water of a mirage does not quench thirst. This world of appearances does not affect the oneness of reality. The mutual deceptive identification of duality and *sat-Brahman* (one-without-a-second existence) is destroyed when they are differentiated. Existence is not two.

It is existence (*sat*) which exists (or is manifested) through all things. These things have no separate existence from existence. That is why existence is One without a Second.

See that'[62]

[62] Inspired by the *The Pançadasi*, by Swami Vidyaranya. Excerpt from *Sâdhus, going beyond the dreadlocks*, by Patrick Levy, Prakash Books, Delhi, 2010.

# V

## Prayers

*Is praying wise? Are prayers of any use? Do they lead to wisdom? Do we find it necessary to ask for God's help because we think he doesn't know what's going on?*
*How does God view prayers? Do they make him happy? Or are prayers a way of trying to experience something of God's depth and intimacy? How do people talk to God? How does God talk to them? And what are we to make of God's silence?*
*Let's look at some inspiring stories about prayers.*

# The evening of Yom Kippur

*'We should pray in such and such a way, and thus serve God because our ancestors also did this.'*
*'But how can you be sure that your ancestors are all in heaven?' replied the Baal Shem Tov.*

It was the evening of Yom Kippur, the day the Jews ask for God's forgiveness...
A Jewish shop keeper wanted to go to the synagogue, an hour's walk from his village, but every time he was about to close his shop, neighbours came in to buy something for the celebration. This meant he couldn't leave.
When he finally managed to close the shop, night had fallen. It was too late. Even if he were to run, he would still arrive at the synagogue after the service had finished. This made him weep bitterly:
'My God, how do I pray to you? I've no knowledge of the prayers.'
However an idea came to him:
'I know the alphabet. So I'll recite the letters, and you shall put them in order. You can make prayers out of them!'[63]

---

63. Variations of this Hassidic tale are told in Jerome Mintz, *Legends of the Hassidim* ; University of Chicago Press, 1974. Harry Rabinovicz, *Hassidism: The Movement and its Masters;* Jason Aronson Inc., 1988. Victor Malka, *Ainsi parlait le hassidisme*, Cerf, 1990.

## Rumi

*A wise man has a sense of humour, and reacts quite freely, even during his conversations with God...*

One day, Rumi, the great Sufi master, was strolling around in order to relax a little. His most devoted disciples followed him, a few paces behind, respecting his solitude. And Rumi was thinking: 'Oh Rumi aren't you doing well? You're dressed in silk, you have new shoes and disciples, ah… things are running nicely for me...'
So God said to him:
'Hey Rumi, would you like me to tell your disciples what you are thinking?'
'Oh no!' Rumi replied. Then, after thinking a little, he added: 'Well, God, they fear and obey you, don't they? Would you like me to tell them about your mercy? Without our misdemeanours, how could you ever make use of your forgiveness?'[64]

[64]. Adapted from Rumi : *In the Arms of the Beloved*, translation John Star, The Putnam Publishing Group, 1997.

## Farewell

*Is it wise to praise the Creator and to glorify him and his name when all around we see the misery and the hardships of living in his Creation? If ever we met with God, face to face, what would we tell him?*

Before he died, the Baal Shem Tov promised his disciples that immediately upon arriving in heaven, he would do everything he could and use all his influence and authority to ensure that the Messiah would be sent to Earth. (The coming of the Messiah on Earth signifies the end of the world and consequently the end of suffering). The very same day, the Baal Shem Tov did actually meet with the Messiah. However the event provoked so much joy in him that he forgot his promise. So the Messiah did not come.

When the Great Maguid had finally reached his dying day he assured everyone that he would be immune to such ecstasy: 'I won't ask to see the Messiah, but I shall pester everyone except him in order to make him come down to the world.' However he made this promise at the beginning of the nineteenth century and the Messiah still has not come.

As for Rabbi Rostrovitch, he didn't promise anything of the sort. He was lying on his bed, dying, when, all of a sudden, gathering what little strength he had left, he stood up, called his disciples and announced to them in a final outburst:

'When I'll appear before God, after my death, I will not let him ask me for an explanation of what I did and did not do. He'll be the one on trial, and I'll be the judge.

I'll tell him: "How can you dare to judge me, I who never asked to be born and am but a tiny creature, while you, who created me and has so much might, have left mankind in misery? What have you been doing for thousands of years? Have you taken a look at the world lately? I've carried the heavy burden of life, and you, were you watching if ever I was about to stumble and fall?"

I'll also tell him: "You have put hell in books and lust in our hearts. What wonder is it then that we are seduced and tempted? We need your mercy before death, not after it."

And I'll add: "Since you dwell in all things, remember that you are also in sin, and most certainly in the sinner."

I won't let up in any way and if he invites me to enter the gates of paradise, to silence me, I won't walk in until all men since the beginning of time are allowed in before me.

My Sons,' he finally told his disciples, 'stop praising or beseeching God. Harass him with your reprimands. That's what he and humanity most need."[65]

[65]. Quotations from Rabbi Lieb, Rabbi Israël of Rijin, the Maguid of Mezeritch; in Harry Rabinovicz, *Hassidism : The Movement and its Masters ; Jason Aronson Inc. ;* 1988. Jerome Mintz, *Legends of the Hassidim* ; University of Chicago Press, 1974. Martin Buber, *Les récits hassidiques*, édition du Rocher, 1963.

## God doesn't need anything

*'He is your praise and He is your God,' the Scriptures tell. Rabbi Pinhas explains this: 'He is your praise, and that's exactly what God is. Prayer is what unites the essences. He who prays knows that his prayer itself is the divine.'* [66]

A disciple of Sheikh Assam devoted himself to prayer from morning till night. He also practiced the meditation of the ninety-nine Names. At night, he read and reread the Holy Koran or practiced zikr - repetitions, in a group. One time during a public meeting, he asked Sheikh Assam:
'I pray more than ten hours every day, and yet I feel no different from before.'
'If you pray for pleasure, continue praying. If you do so as a duty, under some obligation or to please God, then stop. God commands us to pray so that we may find him in ourselves. He doesn't need anything.'
Sheikh Assam then told him this story:
'Every night a man called the name of God ten thousand times: Allah, Allah, Allah, Allah, Allah, Allah, Allah, Allah...
One day, someone said to him:
"Shut up, have you no shame? How long are you going to repeat God's name? Can't you see he isn't answering?"
The man was broken-hearted by these words and fell asleep in that state of mind. Then, in a dream, he saw Elijah, the Prophet, asking him:

[66]. Hassidic tales. *Les récits hassidiques*, édition du Rocher, 1963.

"Why did you stop repeating God's name?"
"I received no answer," the man replied.
Elijah explained:
"God has accepted your prayers. That is why he lets you continue with this activity. The mere fact that you went on praying tells you your prayers are accepted."
God will not appear in your prayers, he is already in them,' said Sheikh Assam. He is *the seeker*. *You cannot find anything that does not already sing His praises*. There is no "outside". No paradise in heaven, no hell elsewhere and no God to be found in someplace else. God is closer to us than our jugular veins. *In fact, he dwells, hidden, between man and his heart*, said the Prophet. We are *the ear with which he hears, the eye with which he sees, the hand with which he strikes, the foot with which he walks.'*

# The Dog and the Cats

*Maybe God is not what we think he is. Repeating praises to the Lord until you get out of breath in order to obtain favours is only rehashing our own wishes. To convey this a sage told the following story:*

One day a wise dog happened to pass by a crowd of cats. As they were all very busy, and since none of them were paying any attention to him, he drew closer.

A large, serious and solemn looking cat, was talking to them in a loud, clear voice: 'Brothers, pray, and when you have prayed, pray again, and you can be sure it will be raining rats.' The dog heard this and laughed to himself. As he sauntered off, he muttered to himself: 'You blind, insane cats, don't you know that it's been written and I myself and my ancestors before me, we've all learnt that through prayer, faith and supplication, it won't be raining rats, but bones!'[67]

[67]. Gibran, *The Madman*, Alfred Knopf, 1949.

## The Alliance

*In 1985, during the ceremony in commemoration of the Holocaust, at the Paris synagogue, the Grand Rabbi Goldman gave a sermon inspired by the resurgence of revisionism.*[68] *He addressed God directly:*
*'Not only did you let your sons be murdered in the Nazi's death camps, but you also let it be said that it didn't even happen! It's as if you were abandoning them a second time... Grant us grace for those who died to pay tribute to your unity, do it for yourself if you don't do it for us, do it for yourself, and give glory to your name.'*[69]
*The Jews have a long tradition of remonstrating God, because they have a sort of contract with him: an Alliance.*

Jacob, the Patriarch, is known to have wrestled with man and with God, and he is said to have prevailed. Since then, some men refuse to bow down before God and his decrees. The Baal Shem Tov, his disciples and their successors were amongst them. They addressed God without obsequiousness and even with some boldness because, according to this tradition, you can freely tell God anything you want, as long as it is in favour of mankind. Uncalled for humility does not honour God.
When misfortune fell upon the country, Rabbi Leib called out to God: 'If you think you'll get your people back to you with

[68]. Revisionism is the denial of the genocide (mass murder) of the European Jews perpetrated by the Nazis during the Second World War.
[69]. « Give us grace... » Psalm 115: 1

pain, I, Leib, son of Rachel, swear that you will not succeed. Save your children with joy, grant them deliverance.'

Rabbi Menachem-Mendel of Kotzk used to say: 'It is written that God saw everything he did and found that it was good. Well I don't.'

As for Rabbi Houne of Kolochitz, he admitted: 'I'm not afraid of anything or anyone, not even an angel, not even God. But the lamentations of a beggar give me the shivers.'

One day, while famine was ravaging the country, the grandfather of Shpole called together a court of ten doctors of the Talmudic law to put God on trial. Thus they rendered their verdict: 'Since a father must feed his children, God is ordered to stop this famine.' When the righteous decides, God must obey.

Regarding Rabbi Levi-Yitzhak of Bertitchev, he went as far as judging and threatening God. He continually reminded God that he too needed to be forgiven: 'There is not a single man before whom God is not guilty.'

'It's in the nature of things that every man pities himself. But now it is time to have pity on God', believed Rabbi Asher of Salouline.[70]

*"As for me, Shahid, I ran away only to tell you that God is crying in my arms." A Gazhal from India.*

---

[70]. Quotation of rabbi Leib, rabbi Menahem-Mendel, rabbi Houne, the grandfather of Shpoie, rabbi Lévi-Yitzhak and of rabbi Acher; in Jerome Mintz, *Legends of the Hassidim*; University of ChicagoPress, 1974. Harry Rabinovicz, *Hassidism : The Movement and its Masters, Jason Aronson Inc.,* 1988. Victor Malka, *Ainsi parlait le hassidisme*, Cerf, 1990. Martin Buber, *Les récits hassidiques*, édition du Rocher, 1963.

## Kabir

*Prayers are sometimes just like testimonies of knowledge, or love songs...*

Since the day when I met my Lord there has been no end to the sport of our love.
I shut not my eyes, I close not my ears, I do not mortify my body;
I see with eyes open, and smile, and behold His beauty is everywhere:
I utter His name, and whatever I do, it becomes His worship.
The rising and the setting are one to me; all contradictions are solved.
Wherever I go, I move round Him,
All I achieve is His service:
When I lie down, I lie prostrate at His feet,
He is the only adorable one to me: I have none other.
My tongue has left off impure words; it sings His glory day and night:
Whether I rise or sit down, I can never forget Him; for the rhythm of His music beats in my ears.
Kabir says: 'My heart is frenzied, and I disclose in my soul what is hidden. I am immersed in that one great bliss which transcends all pleasure and pain.'

There is nothing but water in the holy bathing places; and I know that they are useless, for I have bathed in them.
The images are all lifeless, they cannot speak; I know, for I

have cried aloud to them.
The Purana and the Koran are mere words; lifting up the curtain, I have seen.
Kabir gives utterance to the words of experience; and he knows very well that all other things are untrue.[71]

[71]. *Poems of Kabir*, I 79 and I 76; translated by Rabindranath Tagore; Macmillan Pocket Tagore Edition, India.

## The Atheist and the Devotee

The atheist explained: 'Jesus said: "Truly I say to you: whatever you ask of the Father in my name, He will give it you." That's not true. We all know that it's not true. Actually, this rarely works. So rarely that when it does happen we call it a miracle!

One just has to look around with a little clarity to have some certainty that there is no reason to trust in God. The world is full of misery. Although God is supposed to do everything, he cannot do better and for many it's quite far from enough.'

'When I pray,' replied the devotee, 'I say: "May I be filled with an overflowing love for all creatures; may I be allowed to share all sentient beings' sufferings; may generosity bind me to all those who wander; Bhagwan, O Bhagwan, grant that I may be so!"'[72]

72. Gospel, John 16:23

## Me and You

One night, Bayesid Bestâmi saw the Lord in a dream, who said to him:
'What do you want, Bayesid?'
'Whatever you want for yourself, my Lord!'
'O Bayesid, it's you I want, just like you want me.'
'But,' Bayesid said, 'which road leads to you?'
'O Bayesid! The one who renounces himself will find me.'
From then on, Bayesid Bestâmi prayed to God in the following way:
'How long will there be between you and me, a "*me*" and a "*you*"? Remove from us my "*me*"; let it become entirely your "*you*", and no longer my "*me*".'[73]

*The one who looks upon himself as nothing and aims only to be nothing, this one is a spiritual master, taught the Great Maggid of Mezritch.*

[73]. Liberally adapted from extracts from Bayesid Bestami, in *The Memorial of the Saints, by* Farid-ud-Dun' Attar.

## Silence

*Not everyone prays to the same God; they don't pray in the same way, or for the same reasons... Some don't even pray at all...*

Every morning, he climbed the hill and sat on a stone. Meditating under the shade of the cherry tree he looked around, at the fields, the villages, the cattle, the birds, the blades of grass growing at his feet and the little wild flowers opening slowly... The sky showed him time, the ants activity, men commitment, and the trees patience.
He never prayed. Simply looking at the world was his prayer. Everything he saw was sacred.
Speech makes the world unholy - this is what Silence says.

# VI

## Good and Evil

*What is good and what is evil? What are beauty and ugliness? Such notions are hard to determine.*

*One can marvel at the wonders the world offers for us to enjoy. Yet with a lucid regard one can also see into the horrors contained within some of these wonders.*

*When observed rigorously, nature and life reveal themselves to be appallingly harsh. When volcanoes erupt and kill, when the sick are agonizing and dying, when a butcher cuts a goat's throat to make a feast of its body or a hero kills the enemy, sacrificing his own life for a cause he judges to be right - is any of this good or bad, beautiful or ugly; is it life or death?*

*Men are not the only creatures on Earth. Animals also suffer, live in fear, get eaten by predators who themselves are also prey to other animals. Everything alive lives on the alert. The tiger stalks the antelope, the cat attacks the mouse, the spider on its web waits for the fly... and humans work hard to earn a living and fear bankruptcy or unemployment. Even though we all live in this same world, we don't all have the same role to play. Not every-*

*one manages to find meaning in nature and in society which reveal to us both their faces of wonder and dreadfulness.*

*Injustice, pain, misfortune, the death of children, and of adults, destructive and deadly tidal waves, earthquakes, floods, drought and diseases: what is the meaning behind all this? War, prejudice, fanaticism and crime: why do they exist in this world? And why does hatred exist in our hearts?*

*The wise man has no particular opinion. He simply tries to alleviate suffering and encourage happiness. He relies on what is true and just rather than any notions of good and evil. Whatever arises, he knows that everything has the potential of being an opportunity for learning, and a cause of liberation.*

## What can you do?

A couple of sparrows were nesting above the door of my room, in a hole for an air vent. I was delighted. The sparrows flew in and out of their nest all day long, chattering and fluttering. It made my heart rejoice. One morning, I woke up and to my surprise, caught a cat devouring the two fledglings of the brood which had left the nest for the first time that day. Upon seeing me the cat made off. However one of the fledglings was dead, half eaten, and the other was wounded with a broken wing. I did my best to take care of it. The little sparrow kept on trying to fly off. But to no avail. The exhausting effort was killing it. So I bound it up and placed it in a nest I had made out of old crumpled newspapers, and I left it in a closet with some food nearby. The next day, I discovered that ants had eaten the fledgling alive. All that was left were feathers. 'When you see a fly in a spider's web, what should you do? Leave it alone to be eaten or free it and deprive the spider of its feast?' Swami Vicharava once asked. He then responded to his own question: 'Don't interfere. But take a vow to consume only milk and fruits and avoid becoming a predator yourself.'

*For I do not do the good I want, but I do the very evil I do not want! (Apostle Paul, Romans 7:19)*

## Asanga

*Karuna, compassion or empathy, is one of the two pillars of Buddhism. Karuna is a mental attitude directed towards others, knowing that all sentient beings are subject to suffering as long as they have not reached liberation and enlightenment; it also means doing every possible thing to free them from suffering and attain enlightenment. It's also a type of training: the growing awareness that all beings are like the waves on one, single ocean, or the direct knowledge of the unique and stable consciousness from which everything arises.*

In the solitude of a long retreat in a cave on Gurpa Mountain, Asanga was performing the practices of Maitreya, hoping that through this he would actually meet the Buddha of universal love. After three years of perseverance and diligence, he saw no sign of improvement. Disheartened, he left his retreat and the mountain.

On his way down, he saw a man polishing an iron bar with a cloth.

'What are you doing? he asked him.'

'I am making a needle out of this iron bar, the man replied. I'm polishing it to make it smaller.'

Amazed by the determination of this man, Asanga thought: 'So much ardour for something so unimportant! Compared to this man I certainly lack resolve.' He realized that with such perseverance, he would surely reach enlightenment. So he went back to the cave and resumed his practice of Maitreya's meditation on universal love.

Another three years of retreat passed, and Asanga could not perceive any improvement. Feeling completely discouraged, he once again decided to leave the cave. This time, at the foot of the mountain, he saw a man who was rubbing a huge rock with a feather.

'What are you doing?'

'I'm rubbing this rock to wear it away because it's casting a shadow on my house.'

Once again Asanga was amazed by the man's determination. 'So much effort for such an absurd desire!' he thought. 'To reach enlightenment, I should have even more commitment than this? And it is so much easier!' So he returned to his cave retreat and resumed his practice, meditating on Maitreya for another three years.

Three years later, there was still no sign of change. Completely dejected once again, he left his cave. On his way down the mountain, he met an old crippled dog whose body was covered with wounds infected by worms. A deep compassion for the dog arose in him, and he wished to help it. But he also felt great compassion for the worms. If he tried to remove them with his fingers, he would crush them, and if he left them on the ground, they would die. So, he cut a large piece of flesh from his thigh to put them on, and with the hope that he could remove them with his tongue without harming them, he overcame his disgust, closed his eyes and leaned forward to lick.

At that moment he realized he had reached his goal.[74]

[74]. A Tibetan tale told during a teaching by Kalu Rinpoche.

# The Brahmin and the Prostitute

A Brahmin and a prostitute were neighbours living in the same street. The Brahmin was very famous for his devotion; he was known for performing endless rituals all day long. He lived a life of penance and austerities. He never laughed. He thought of himself as a great saint and taught devotees a path leading to God paved with nothing but sacrifice and surrender.

The prostitute was selling her body in order to survive.

One day the Brahmin went to her house to give her a sermon: 'You are a great sinner,' he said. 'Your evil deeds are accumulating; a dreadful fate awaits you after death.'

The poor woman repented wholeheartedly. She begged for forgiveness from God; however with no other means of livelihood she had no choice but to carry on her work. But there was never a moment that she stopped begging and imploring God for forgiveness.

The Brahmin and the Prostitute died the very same day.

Yama, the Lord of death, came for the woman's soul and led her on the way to heaven whilst demons arrived to take hold of the Brahmin's soul and throw it into hell.

'What is this?' the Brahmin screamed. 'There must be a mistake. I have lived a holy life. Why should I go to hell while this woman who lived a life of sins is taken to heaven?'

'Because,' the demons answered, 'this woman was selling her body, but she was always thinking of God and begging his pardon. You, on the contrary, when you were performing your devotions, your mind was always fixed on your neighbour's sins. All you could see were sins, you thought of nothing but sins, so now you're going where sinners go.'[75]

*'Our thoughts more than our actions determine what we become'. Ramakrishna*

[75]. A tale from India.

# Kali

In the days when the universe was created Kali, the dreadful demon, asked Parikshit, the King of the Earth, where his place on Earth was to be.
'There is no place for you on earth,' Parikshit replied.
But Kali begged him:
'Don't be so cruel. You are justice and mercy, have mercy on me. I need a shelter.'
So Parikshit offered him bars, brothels, gaming rooms and slaughterhouses. Kali bowed and thanked him but still begged for other places he could inhabit. Parikshit gave him lies, pride, passion, ignorance and hostility. Kali bowed but insisted, 'Isn't there some prestigious place for me in this world?' 'Dwell in gold! Gold ruins men,' the King of the Earth finally conceded.

# The Robber of Speech

One day, Pranesh, an honourable thief belonging to the honourable caste of thieves, met Kundapura, an honourable merchant belonging to the honourable caste of merchants. They conversed about the merits of their respective professions:
'Stealing for a living seems very risky to me' said Kundapur-the-merchant. 'Inevitably, one day someone will catch you, and your victims will demand revenge and justice!'
'Stealing is more than a job, it's an art,' replied Pranesh-the-thief, nobly. 'Since the beginning of time, initiations in the art of stealing have been passed down in our family from father to son: the art of stealing without being seen, the art of stealing without having to flee, the art of slipping away, if necessary, from perilous situations, and the art of stealing without ever having to lie.'
'What! you steal but you won't lie!' Kundapura-the-merchant exclaimed. 'That beats everything. In business, we do the opposite. We never steal anything of course, but as for exaggerating on the merits of a product, as for giving slender rice instead of long rice, lying about the quality of lentils, fiddling with the scales, or selling gold plated metal and sometimes even copper for pure gold... well, you know you have to make a living!'
'If that's so,' Pranesh-the-thief replied angrily, 'you're more than a thief, more than a bandit, more than a crook... you're a cheat! When I steal something, I take what I take but no more than that. Whereas when you lie, you steal speech, and

stealing that, you take, destroy and annihilate the whole universe.'

And he quoted the scriptures:

"'All things are determined by speech. Speech is the root of everything, everything proceeds from it. The one who is dishonest with respect to speech, is dishonest in everything.'"[76]

[76]. The Law of Manou IV : 256.

## Good versus Evil

*You have heard that it was said, 'You shall love your neighbour and hate your enemy.' But I tell you, 'love your enemies and bless those who curse you, do good to those who hate you'. Matthew 5: 43-44*

In the evening, father Guichard was in the cafe reading the newspaper with a few of his parishioners.
That day, two news items had caught his attention. The first: three men had stolen the cash from a bank cashier at gun point. The second: two hitchhikers had robbed a man who had agreed to take them in his car.
The priest was asked what he thought of this. He replied:
'Here I see two very different crimes.
The first is an offence against property. That's obvious. The gangsters did not hide their intentions. Banks are prepared for this kind of misfortune and holdups actually help them to improve their security.
The second is a crime against hospitality and this offence is worse than the attack on the bank. The generous driver offered the asylum of his car; he was led to believe that he was helping people in need of transportation. He was doing good and was a factor in contributing in spreading it. Robbing him, his assailants have stolen much more than the wallet of their host; they stole goodness itself from everyone.
Evil isn't measured in terms of the cost of damages but in the cost of consequences. In this case what are they? This driver will no longer take hitchhikers, and those who are informed of

his misfortune will now become reluctant to offer hospitality to strangers.

Whoever responds to good with evil destroys the impulse of generosity and the ideal of sharing; he weakens trust, and inhibits its impetus. He gives selfishness a justification it doesn't need. To return good with evil is more than a misdemeanour, it's an aberration.'

'Father, will you still take in hitchhikers?'

'Of course! If we are suspicious of all strangers, how can we practice charity? And who will help us when we need help? In fighting evil there is nothing other than good.'

## A Lesson in Governing

Once upon a time, the King of Kosala, with his coach and retinue came across the King of Kashi's coach and retinue on a narrow road. There was insufficient room for both coaches to pass each other.

'Get out of the way!' shouted the driver of the King of Kosala to the driver of the King of Kashi.

'No, you should back up!' shouted the other driver.

'I'm driving the King of Kosala!'

'And I'm driving the King of Kashi! Get out of the way.'

They tried to find a way to solve their dispute. The driver of the King of Kashi inquired about the age of the King of Kosala, but they were both born in the same year. They tried to decide according their caste and their families, but they were equal in honour and reputation. Furthermore both were loved by their subjects.

'What are the moral qualities of your master?' then asked the King of Kashi's driver to his colleague from Kosala.

'He is tough with the thugs and gentle with the mild. He is kind to good people and obnoxious with bad ones.'

'How great his vices must be if they are a measure of his virtues!' said the driver of the King of Kashi. 'My king conquers anger with kindness, evil with good, greed with generosity. And to lies he answers only with the truth.'

When he heard these words the King of Kosala alighted from his coach and ordered his men to clear the way.[77]

---

77. From The Jakata, the legends of Buddha.

## Satan was a saint

One day, Allah made plans to create a man on earth. He informed his angels, but they responded by disparaging his intentions:

'You are about to create someone who will sow scandal and shed blood whereas we glorify Your praise and proclaim Your holiness!'

'I know what you don't know,' Allah told them.

Once he had created the first man, Allah commanded his angels to prostrate before this man. Everyone obeyed this order except Satan, who refused, saying:

'I am not the kind to bow before a man.'

'What stops you from prostrating when I order you to? Allah asked him.

Satan knew that God is One, that He has no equal, and that no one should prostrate himself before anybody else but Him... even when ordered by Him.

'I am much better than a man,' Satan answered. 'You created me from fire and him from clay. You will not find any gratitude either in him or the majority of his descendants.'

So, Allah banished him:

'You cannot stay here with such pride. Get out of my sight! You are now among the lesser beings.'

Upon hearing this condemnation, Satan said:

'Even if I am cursed in both worlds, the fire of love burning in me won't lose its ardour. I'll never bow before any other than Allah himself, even if it means being damned for eternity. But because you demean me, I'll rule over the descendants of the one you honour more than me. I'll be watching out for them, I'll walk before and behind them, I'll be to their right and to their left.'

Since that time, Satan is deemed to be responsible for the downfall of humanity and to be the cause of evil and sin.

But, let us remember for now that it was because of his love for Allah that Satan refused to honour a man, and that, to prove his loyalty, he refused to concede. His love and devotion were perfect and unmitigated, and even his sentence of eternal banishment did not make him waiver. Who can boast of such devotion? Even the greatest saints grow dim in comparison.[78]

[78]. Kuran 7: 10-17; 17: 62. From an idea by Farid-ud-din Attar.

## Do it for no reward

*Renouncing all attachment to the fruits of his action, ever satisfied, without seeking support or protection, depending on nothing, and even though he is engaged in action, he does absolutely nothing, the Bhagavad Gita teaches.*

A temple was being built in the Buddhist Centre... Disciples, visitors and friends were invited to lend a hand in its construction: 'A temple lasts one thousand years. Those who help building it will acquire merits and positive karma for one thousand years!' the Rinpoche promised the crowd of helpers who were delighted to believe they were ensuring themselves happiness in future lives in return for some hard physical work, without having to do any real work on themselves, or making any deep spiritual transformation.

A disciple who was a bit wiser than the others went and saw the Rinpoche privately, and he told him:

'Helping out in the construction of the temple is certainly a positive effort and sometimes it's even fun, but doing it for "merit" or some benefit in a future life, isn't that a little petty? One who accomplishes a good deed for a salary, out of interest for an immediate profit or a future reward, gives his act the value he expects from it. However an act accomplished without expectations of payment or reward becomes priceless and has an infinite value. You should invite everyone to participate in the construction of the temple for nothing, no rewards, no future positive karma, because for nothing, the act becomes a true gift and contains unlimited merit! The greater good is one for which you expect nothing, because it doesn't bind the one who receives it, and it frees the one who does it.'

The master agreed:

'Some do it for money, others do it for merit, others for pride, and others out of friendship. Everyone does what he can... But doing it for nothing is better, of course.' And he added with some hypocrisy: 'Don't tell the others. To get to the summit of a mountain there are many paths.'

*In Tibetan Buddhism a practice begins and ends with a dedication:*

*'May the virtuous activity produced by the practice of giving and other perfections produce enlightenment for the benefit of all beings.'*

*'By the virtue that I created in performing this action, may I establish all beings without exception beyond suffering. I dedicate all merits to the attainment of enlightenment.'*

*The wish for enlightenment is not for oneself but for all beings, so it continues to be an unselfish wish which means that wish can become a seed of freedom, and thus a cause of enlightenment.*

# The alms

*When you give change to a beggar, don't ask yourself whether or not he deserves it, if he will use it "well" or not. Who knows who is good or bad? Be like God who causes the sun to rise on the evil and the good, and sends rain on the righteous and the unrighteous.*

Wu Ho, a poor and hungry man, saw that the monks of the nearby monastery were receiving alms. Not only did laymen give generously to those wearing the robes of the religious order, but they also showed them respect and even reverence. But to Wu Ho, they gave nothing.

The monks often handed out some of their food to the poor, but the poor were many and Wu Ho only rarely received anything.

One day, Wu Ho put on a monk's robe and therefore received his share of offerings and consideration. He continued this until one day he really decided to become a monk. He asked for ordination and became an ardent devotee. He was a disciple of Yuan Ki Tzu.

One winter morning, Wu Ho and his master, Yuan Ki Tzu, were walking along a road under the cold rain. They came across a beggar and gave him all the food they had. They saw another beggar and offered him all the money they had. They met a man shivering with cold and gave him their blankets.

As they arrived in a village they went knocking on doors to beg for alms.

'Master, why do we give everything we own if afterwards we

must go and beg,' Wu Ho asked?
'We are monks,' Yuan Ki Tzu replied, 'and we have taken a vow to live on alms only. We act according to our commitment when we beg. We have also taken the vow not to own anything. So, we also act according to our commitment when we give away whatever we receive.'
Wu Ho understood there and then the meaning of the vows he had taken and he said:
'That's right, master. Lay people choose whom they offer their good deeds to. They give more generously to monks, so in turn we distribute what they give us.'
He bowed to his master, and then added:
'All we own is our vows. They are our real masters.'

*Love does not choose. God dwells in everyone. Feeding others without choosing to whom we offer our help is the same as serving God, said Ramakrishna.*

# The Man who threw the stone and the Man who received it

A king was taking a rest in an orchard, accompanied by his governors and courtiers. A poor man passed by. He was unaware of both the king and his courtiers and only saw the orchard's trees laden with their ripe fruit. He was very hungry. He threw a stone into a mango tree. Three delicious mangoes fell to the ground which he then picked up.

However the stone that he had thrown fell and struck the king on his head.

The guards and courtiers were quick to find the man who they thought had made an attempt on their king's life. They seized him and, and without further ado, wishing to show the extent of affection they had for their king, sentenced him to death on the spot.

But the king, who was just and wise, objected:

'This poor and hungry man threw a stone into a mango tree to get some of its fruits and eat them. The mango tree gave him some. From a tree, which has no compassion, he has obtained enough to eat for a day. Would a man endowed with compassion give him any less?'

He then gave an order to his minister of the treasury:

'From today until the end of his life this man must receive one gold coin every week.'[79]

---

[79]. Adapted from a story told by Swami Sivananda, *Inspiring Stories*, Divine Life Society Publication, Sivanandanagar, UP, 1997.

## Solidarity

A missionary was in Africa to preach the gospel, teach about good and evil and his knowledge of God. His job was to take care of the children; he taught them the catechism and was also their gym teacher.

One morning, bringing a box of chocolates with him to school he prompted his pupils to make a running race. He said to the children:

'Look at that tree over there. When I count to three, you must run as fast as you can. The first to get to the tree will be the winner and will win this box of chocolates.'

He counted to three to give the starting signal. Then the kids, instinctively, without saying anything to each other, took hold of each other's hands and ran together arriving at the tree at the same time.

What do these kids understand that we don't? What were they told from infancy that made them refuse to compete if there are winners and losers? They saw themselves to be responsible for each other's happiness. Can we follow them and do the same? Are we able to hold each other's hand and ensure that there are no losers in this world?[80]

[80]. An anecdote told by Raymon Panikkar.

## Spread whatever good fortune has given you

*Rumi was walking in broad daylight holding a lighted lantern in his hand. When questioned by the passers-by about this strange behaviour, he replied: 'I am looking for a living man who has the spirit of a saint.'*

A volunteer working for a NGO was interviewed by a reporter.

'What motivates you in your work? Do you believe in God? Do you have political ideals?'

'No,' replied the volunteer. 'You don't try to help the poor and work against destitution to glorify God, spread an ideology or build your self esteem, but rather to face your fears, your helplessness and limitations. The poor show us that our well-being is fragile, and that tragedies happen suddenly and unexpectedly.

Our good fortune for being well off, having life's necessities and even more than we need, for being healthy and safe, loved and respected, carries a duty: it chooses us so that we give it a life and spread it. Of course, luck is not a person and has no will of its own. It's a concept we use to say that we have given up trying to explain why fate or destiny has given us a life in a prosperous family, in a country at peace, in overall happier circumstances than others... Though it is inexplicable, what chance has given us holds a potentially infinite multiplier. If the one who has, gives a little of what he has, if the one who is able, helps a little, if those who know something teach what they know, and if those who are given, helped and taught, give, help and teach others in turn, obeying the same duty, then there will no more poor and suffering around us.

When it is intentionally spread and multiplied, luck goes beyond the narrow realm of chance, and proliferates until it touches everyone. It lives and thrives, fertilized by charity which is a way of creating the justice that luck cannot establish.'

# Do unto your neighbour…

My travelling companion and I were waiting along the burning hot asphalt of a dusty road for a bus to take us anywhere. Some were passing by, but they were all completely full, as buses can be in India, packed with people right up to the door.

The sun was biting our flesh, the dry heat weighed heavier on our shoulders than our backpacks, the dust was making breathing a painful activity and the brightness irritated our eyes. We were tired. Through seeing the unrelenting indifference of the bus drivers ignoring us, our sense of humour had long vanished. Hours were also passing by and soon night would fall…

A bus, just as crowded as the others, finally stopped. The front door opened, and jammed packed passengers squashed themselves into spaces where there had previously been none, generously creating enough room to welcome us with kindness and understanding. We drove off. We were finally going somewhere, albeit very slowly.

The engine was overheating. Crushed on my companions, I was suffocating, I needed air. I was rapidly growing weaker and I felt like I was going to faint very soon. How long could I hold on?

Through the windscreen I noticed two men with their bundle by the roadside waiting for a bus and I surprised myself wishing that the bus wouldn't stop! Yet I had been in the exactly the same situation less than ten minutes before. The bus went past them, but I immediately felt sorry about it.

Further along, two women with their bundles were waiting by

the road. I shouted out, as one can do in India, for the driver to stop. He stopped. And there I was even more crushed, but happy to be sharing the relief of these two unknown women that circumstance had squashed up against me in a happy, innocent and unintentional embrace.

"Go ahead and convert me, but on the condition that you teach me the whole Bible in the time I can stand on one foot," said a pagan to Rabbi Shammai. Rabbi Shammai drove him away, hitting him with a builder's ruler that he was holding. The man then went to Rabbi Hillel, who converted him saying: 'Don't do to your neighbour what you wouldn't want him to do to you. This sums up the whole Bible. The rest is just comments. Go and study them.'

Later, Jesus made an improvement to this principle: 'Do to others what you would have them do to you.'[81]

[81]. Quotation from the Talmud of Babylon, Chabbat 31a. Then Matthew 7:12.

# VII

## Real or Illusion?

*One day, Darwin was visiting the aborigines, accompanied by a pastor who held a Bible in his hand. 'An aboriginal stood there staring at the object in the pastor's hand. He had no means of understanding what it was', Darwin commented, 'because he had no framework or reference that might give it meaning. He had no idea of what writing or a book was and even less of what the Bible represented.'*

*Plato's 'myth of the Cave' demonstrated how appearances can be deceptive. Schopenhauer added: 'The world is my representation. Everything that exists, exists in my mind.' And Nietzsche stated that 'we live only through illusions. Many things elude our attention. Our awareness only touches the surface of things.'*

*When I observe, I observe through a filter. I never see 'what is' but only what the filter allows me to perceive. This filter is made of the senses' inherent limits, but also the limits of my knowledge, my memory, my conditioning, my culture, my habits and even my mood. This filter is me. The observer believes he is different from what he perceives, but in fact, he sees himself through what is perceived.*

*So what is reality? Is there a way to know? Can wisdom be found through trying to answer these questions?*

## The Wisdom of Enlightenment

Master Takuan was lying on the futon, in his empty room. He was dying. A disciple approached him and asked him what his last will would be. Takuan said he didn't have one. However the disciple insisted:

'Surely you must have something to say?'

'Life is a dream,' the master replied. And he told this story:

"A man yearned to be rich. Every day he would go to the temple and pray that God bestow wealth upon him. One winter day, returning from the temple, he saw a fat wallet frozen into the ice. He immediately thought his prayers had finally been answered. Since he couldn't pull the wallet free from the ice, he urinated on it... And suddenly he awoke in his wet bed."

This is how our life is,' Master Takuan added. 'Don't expect miracles like the man who urinated in his bed. Don't seek a state of transcendental consciousness. Wisdom is not miraculous; awakening is not a special condition of the mind, it means to be awakened to our life, it's as simple as that.'

And he died.[82]

*'We are what we think. Everything we are arises with our thoughts. With our thoughts we make the world. Mind is the source of every kind of knowledge'. Buddha.*[83]

[82]. A tale from Japan. *Record of Takuan, Zen record of Takuan sensei*, Kyoto 1974.

[83]. Buddha, Dhammapada, I, 1.

## Where am I?

It is told that Tupala was a great king who was devoted to his subjects, generous towards the Brahmins*, gentle with children, respectful of wise men and wisdom and who followed the rules of good governance.

One hunting night, leaving his retinue far behind, he ventured far and deep into the forest and lost his way.

At dawn, he arrived in front of a hut where an untouchable was cleaning out the carcass of a bull. As he was surprised to find himself there, the King was about to ask where he was and in which province and hamlet he had arrived, when he caught sight of a dazzlingly beautiful young girl. She was simple and smiling, the very embodiment of grace. And of course he fell in love with her.

At the speed of an arrow piercing through space, he forgot about the hunting, his kingdom and government. He was treated with familiarity as if he had been long awaited. He married the girl, and with her came the tannery, the livestock and the forest, the adobe house which had to be patched up after rain, the herd of buffaloes that need taking to the pasture in the morning and bringing back at night, the harvests and monsoon seasons, rough clothes and rope beds... He embraced the worship of the forest Gods and joined with the villagers in prayer. He experienced the peace that follows a hard day's work, and suffered the anxieties of waiting for rain.

His wife gave him a son, then a second one, and then a third. He lived through seasons of happiness and years of misfortune. Sickness took away his eldest son, then his father-in-law, whom he replaced as a tanner. Then came a year of scarcity after a year of drought, and another there was a great flood, which swept away the cattle. During one monsoon, his beloved wife drowned in the lake. Years had passed, and yet more followed.

One evening, exhausted, he fell asleep in the grasslands and dreamed a strange dream that he was a just and good king, governing his kingdom. One hunting night, he lost his way in the forest, arrived in front of a hut, saw a stunningly beautiful girl, forgot his palace and married her, became a tanner after the death of his father-in-law, lost his eldest son to sickness, then his cattle in a flood, and then his wife drowned in a lake... One day, his Prime Minister appeared there, in his courtyard, and threw himself at his feet.

'Majesty, we have been searching for you unceasingly all this time; we have scoured the entire kingdom, from North to South and even the outer provinces to the smallest hamlets; we have covered and searched this vast jungle without rest! Thank God we have finally found you!'

As the king was returning to his capital, escorted by his guards and his Prime Minister, he woke up, astounded to find himself in his palace bed.

It had been a dream.

It had all been nothing but a dream, but this dream had had the taste, colour, texture and charm of reality. During this sleep, the king felt perfectly awake, exactly as he was now.

At this moment who was he? A king in his palace, the tanner in the dream or the sleeping tanner now dreaming that he is a king? Or perhaps even someone else, sleeping somewhere in a distant universe about which he had forgotten everything, and who was dreaming that he was dreaming that he was dreaming... And what of the small house in the forest, and the untouchable, his wonderful wife, the buffalo herd, the rough bed, and his sons, the sickness and the drowning? Were these last years merely a few hours in one night? And is life just a moment of dreaming in eternity? Are we but characters in the dream of a sleeping man? When can one know what is true? When does one wake up? Is truth just a word to be found in the humdrum of confusion or is it the continual and indivisible flow of thoughts and dreams?

In the morning, he left his palace in a palanquin carried by four strong Brahmins. One of them, uncaring and unconcerned, carried it so roughly, bumping here and stumbling there, that the king could bear no more of it and leapt out to scold him: 'Who are you? And why are you so clumsy?'

'My King, I am tall and fat and rather ugly and I am a Brahmin, but tell me, who am I really? And you, who are you? What can you be called? Are you your body? Are you your birth? And why are you a king? Where does this palanquin come from, do you know? Which kind of wood is it made of? Was the tree already a palanquin in the forest? And was the cotton flower already this robe that you are wearing? The air is everywhere, and yet when one blows a little of it in a flute, as it passes through the holes it produces a "la", a "so" or a "re" and finally a melody. In just the same way there is neither a 'me' nor a 'you', but only one existence in the endless flow of life.'

Having heard this, the king felt the power of truth in his heart, beating faster and harder, and was instantaneously freed from

birth and the belief in an existence.
The instant of a flash of lightening is all it takes to awaken to truth. Then, all we have to do is go there, where there is neither identity nor the possibility of losing it, neither existing nor the memory of existence, neither birth nor the fatality of death, as if one is endlessly awakening from having passed out and incessantly asking oneself: *where am I*?[84]

[84]. Two stories of the Hindu mythology, liberally adapted from Vasista Ramayana and Bhagavatham.

## Zhuangzi

*Life may be nothing but a dream, but who is doing the dreaming?*

One night, Zhuangzi dreamt that he was a butterfly flitting and fluttering around, satisfied with life and doing as he pleased, not knowing he was Zhuangzi. Suddenly he woke up and there he was, surprised to be Zhuangzi.
At that point he questioned whether he was Zhuangzi who had dreamt he was a butterfly, or a butterfly now dreaming himself to be Zhuangzi.[85]

*Whether Zhuangzi is dreaming that he is a butterfly or a butterfly is dreaming he is Zhuangzi, do we not find wisdom in simply knowing we are dreaming?*

[85]. Zhuangzi.

## What never changes?

*In Eastern philosophy, only that which is permanent can be called 'real', that which doesn't change or is beyond change. But what is it that never changes?*

A Guru and his disciple had been practicing meditation for many years sitting silently in front of the Ganges. Every morning, they offered garlands of flowers to the sacred river. One day the Guru asked the disciple:
'What never changes?'
The disciple thought about it for a while and reflected upon each of the things he saw or did… 'The flowers that I have offered today are different from those I offered yesterday. Have I, myself not changed a little since yesterday? My Guru is getting older. Every day I pray, but never in exactly the same way.'
He saw the corpse of a dead sadhu floating along the river's current. 'Life is fleeting, death takes it away one day. And the water, even the water from Ganges passes and is always different, but…
'The current! The current in Ganges is always there! Whatever its strength, it's always there!' the disciple exclaimed.
'A good answer' the master replied. 'It's faster during the monsoon, slower in the dry season, but it's always there in the river bed.'
The next day, during his meditation, the disciple was still looking for what never changes. He pondered upon everything he saw: 'The caterpillar becomes a butterfly. The sun does not

rise at the exact same place, yet it rises every day, and whilst the moon doesn't have the same aspect every night, it is in the sky every night... Every day I'm hungry, even though we don't always have food. Some people are generous, others give us nothing, yet sometimes someone who usually gives us nothing, gives alms. Nothing is really ever certain...'

The disciple turned to his Guru and said:

'What never changes is that everything changes all the time.'

'A good answer,' the Guru replied without moving. 'Everything changes all the time! Everything-changes-all-the-time is permanent, unchanging, eternal, immortal... And as we also change, we participate in the ongoing current of transformation of everything. But there is yet something else that does not change: that which is never affected by changes is our perfect acceptance of change.'[86]

*Heraclitus also said, 'We never bathe twice in the same river.'*

[86]. Jacques Laffitte, *Petits Contes de la Vie et de ce qui s'ensuit.*

# The rope and the snake

*Is there a world? Is it real or is it only a perception of something else?*

One evening, Naraya was walking in a forest. Suddenly in the twilight, he noticed a snake. His heart skipped a beat and he quickly ran away. Later that evening, he brought a lamp and, investigating more carefully, he discovered that what he had mistaken for a snake was in fact a rope, nothing more than a rope…

Prassad knew this story. One day he rushed to his master and out of breath he proclaimed,

'I was walking through the jungle, and I saw a dead branch lying on the ground. I thought it was a snake.'

'Why are you terrified by such an insignificant thing?' the master replied. 'Don't you know the secrets of Maya?'

'Well, I had a real fright when I picked the branch up… It was a snake!'[87]

*We perceive events, but our perception and our understanding don't guarantee us that these events really and only exist as we believe they do.*

[87]. On an idea of Anthony de Mello

# The mirror

*There are no facts, Nietzsche said, only interpretations.*

An old Tibetan farmer went to town to sell his harvest. As he had done good business, he spent some time walking through the market, until a salesman showed him a mirror. He had no real idea of what it was, but when he looked into it, he saw his father. Feeling moved, he bought it.

Back home, he placed the mirror in a chest in his bedroom. Whenever he was overcome by nostalgia, he would enter his room, and alone, he would open the chest and gaze at his father.

One day his wife caught sight of him playing this little game. So when the farmer was out in the fields, she opened the chest and saw... a woman! Mad with jealousy, she scolded her husband when he came back. They were still quarrelling when a nun passed by. So the husband and wife took her as arbitrator.

'Wait,' she said, 'I'll go see for myself.'

She opened the chest, peered into it, turned around and then said:

'There is nothing to worry about, she's a nun!'

# The Jinx

*Surely, the world is more complex and subtle than what I am capable of perceiving but how can I be aware of what I'm missing? Could it be that it is the object of a belief? Are we responsible for what we believe in or are we simply the playthings of our beliefs?*

One day two of my friends were arguing. Elizabeth was accusing Veronica of having the evil eye and of putting jinxes on others. How does anyone go about refuting such an accusation? Veronica was astounded.

They were quarrelling over this until they took me as an arbitrator. Having heard the reprimands of one and the denials of the other, I told them:

'Listen. There is no such a thing as an evil eye. Stop being ridiculous.'

A few months later, as Swami Vicharava had been talking about the occult forces at work in the world, I told him about the dispute between Elizabeth and Veronica and my reaction. He said:

'It was Elizabeth who was jinxing Veronica and not the contrary because her accusation of bringing bad luck was an imposition that was a jinx in itself. She was imprisoning Veronica in a fate from which she couldn't escape.'

Swamiji smiled and added:

'You should have told Veronica to cast a spell on Elizabeth!'

This time it was me who was startled. Swamiji explained:

'By threatening her with a curse, Veronica would have forced

Elizabeth to reconsider whether she really wanted to grant her this sort of power or ascendancy over her. A spell only works when someone believes in it. So the curse would have imprisoned the one who had the possibility of lifting it, Elizabeth, rather than the one who was supposed to be under it, Veronica. And Elizabeth would have had to verify at her own risk whether or not Veronica's jinx was real.'

In the naval cemetery of Saint-Louis in Senegal, I met a marabout. Since we were talking about spirits, I told him the story of Veronica. He said:

'I wouldn't have handled this matter so lightly. I would have said: "Veronica has nothing to do with it! She is possessed by an evil spirit." And I would have made a spell to free her. Then both Veronica and Elizabeth would have been rid of it.'

## The Kabbalist

*Kabbalah is a method of metaphysical speculation based on the meaning of Hebrew letters, words and numbers and their correlations. It is an attempt to unravel the mysteries of how this world came into being, giving an account of the causal chain, consisting of forces and properties, which allows the infinite to limit itself in creation and man to exist in separation from his creating cause.*

'Come and see,' Rabbi Isaac said.

'The Bible opens with this verse: "*Berechit*, in the beginning, created Elohim the heavens and the earth". The tradition allows us to recombine the letters of a word to extract more meaning from it. In this way the reading of the Bible is constantly renewed through commentaries. The Zohar teaches *that* the two syllables of the name of the Creator God, Elohim, can be read, first in the right way, and secondly in reverse: Elohim gives *Eleh-mi*. "*Mi* (who) is associated with *Eleh* (that) to compose the word Elohim," it is said. "This name is never broken up and it is from this intimacy that the world endures" our masters taught. "*Who* is the extreme upper limit of questioning, *That*, is its lower limit," it is said. "*Who* is the very heart of thinking and questioning, existing and nonexistent..." When *Who* and *That* are together there is a unified reality.

"In the beginning *Who* and *That* (Elohim) created the heavens and the earth," it is written. "The heavens and earth" means everything, the Totality. When you separate *Who* and *That* you break this totality, the unity of the cause is split, and you separate yourself from everything. You acquire your own existence and a creation exists for you because you are separated from it. If you understand that you conceive yourself, you move up one step in the causal ladder. If you think of yourself as essence, you still move up. At the top of the ladder there is the *Ayn-Sof*, the Without-end, the Infinite. Here, all questions vanish in the unseparated consciousness of Elohim. Here, reality doesn't exist any more than you do.'

Going over his explanation once again, as was his wont, Rabbi Isaac said:

'And see this also: '*Who created That*,' said the prophet Isaiah. If you it read as a question, you separate *Who* and *That*; so you have to create a religion to reconnect yourself to what you yourself have dissociated from. If you read it as an affirmation *Who* and *That* are already together and you enter into the unified and impersonal awareness of the divinity itself: *Who* is therefore the subject, the creator, inseparable from *That*, the Creation, because there is no Creator without a Creation. This is what brings light to the worlds.

But there is still something more: "He hung the earth upon the *not-that, emptiness, the void*, as it is written in the book of Job. Everything dwells on nothingness."[88]

[88]. The interpretation of the name *Elohim* in Zohar, Preliminaries 2a and 1b. "*Who created That*": Isaiah 40: 26. Then "*He hung the earth on nothing*": Job 26: 7.

# VIII

## Death

*Death is a subject of concern for everyone: men and women, believers and non-believers, all casts and classes, the young and the old, wise men, lay men, the ignorant - everybody. Although some live longer than others, no one escapes it. Thus, Death is Equality's attendant. Everything is finally reduced to this same fate. It is an absolute value in a transient world.*

*Death is a very serious problem - we will die one day. Yet it shows us that nothing is really very serious, precisely because everything, absolutely everything will disappear. Not just living beings but also objects, mountains, planets. Even Gods perish: no one worships Mazda or Zeus or Ra anymore! Paul Valéry established that civilizations are mortal. Since then, astrophysicists and ecologists have taught us that the planet we live on is mortal as well. Even worse, the universe itself is subject to the law of impermanence.*

*Everything dies.*

*'Death is the only truth,' asserted Lacan. 'These same young people who are afraid of life will later be afraid of*

*death,' remarked C.G Jung. 'The only evil is death!' said one of the Karamazov brothers. And Malraux: 'Death is the only certainty that brings no peace of mind.' But Thomas Bernhard replies: 'The thought that life ends definitely is beautiful.' And Borges: 'Freed from the masks that I was, I shall be in death pure forgetfulness.'*
*What do the wise say about this thing from which no one escapes?*

## A Handful of Rice

A widow hurried to meet the Buddha with her only child, lying dead in her arms. With this loss, she had lost her reason to live.

'Bring him back to life,' she begged the Awakened one.

But the Buddha never performed this sort of miracle. Instead he said to the widow:

'Go to the village and bring me back a handful of rice from a house where no one ever died.'

The woman went knocking on doors, visiting every house in the village. 'We can give you rice, but my father died here last year...' 'Our son was struck by illness and he died three months ago...' 'Many members of my family died in this house during the year of the drought...' were the replies she received.

She went everywhere, but nowhere did she find a house where no one had ever died. Night soon fell.

Wandering alone, empty-handed, on the dirt roads she thought to herself: 'Death took my husband and then my only child; one day it will take me as well. What happened to my son is not such an unusual tragedy.' She understood: 'Death is part of life; it comes to everyone.'

She buried her child, returned to the Buddha and became his disciple.[89]

---

[89]. A Buddhist wisdom tale.

## The Most Extraordinary Fact

*Nobody will escape death, but who is really willing to believe it?*

Yudhishthira and his four brothers, fleeing their enemies, had walked all day long without drinking and were very thirsty. When they finally took a moment to rest, Sahadeva, the younger of the Pandavas, went in search of water. He came upon a lake. When he bent to drink, a *Yaksha* appeared:
'If you drink before you answer my questions, you will die,' threatened the spirit of the lake.
Yet Sahadeva did not wait, he drank the water and died.
The three other brothers came in search of him, yet they too encountered the *Yaksha* and ended up suffering the same fate.
Then Yudhishthira, the eldest who was known for his wisdom, on seeing that his brothers had not returned, went to explore the surroundings where he found the lake, his four lifeless brothers and the *Yaksha*.
'Your brothers died because they refused to answer my questions,' said the spirit.
'Ask your questions then,' consented Yudhishthira.
The *Yaksha* asked more than one hundred questions. Then finally, it asked:
'What is the most extraordinary fact of life?'
Yudhisthira looked at the bodies of his four brothers and understanding what had happened to them said:
'Everyone is subject to death. Tens of thousands of men and women die every day, yet those who are still alive believe

themselves to be beyond death's reach. This is the most extraordinary fact of life.'[90]

*Man on earth believes himself to be above everything. Once he is in the earth does he know that he is less than nothing?*

90. Mahabharata

## The Disease

The doctor told him his illness was fatal; there was nothing in science or medicine that could do anything to prevent it developing.

'How much longer have I got?'

'A few months. Between three and twelve.'

First, he refused this brutal and fatal diagnosis, constantly repeating in his mind: "No, not me, not to me! This only happens to others. Death can't come to me yet.' But soon enough he realized that he was a human being like everyone else, and that others too have died at an early age, that anyone could become sick and die. Death is the universal fate. 'But, not now, not yet…'

A few weeks later, he wondered: 'Why me, why now? What have I done to deserve this?' But he soon realized that there were numerous explanations with no right answer to these questions. For a while he entertained the idea that the doctors were wrong, he wouldn't die. He tried to negotiate with them: 'Couldn't it be that I'll live another year or maybe even two? You'll see, I be cured! I feel better sometimes.' But he could not escape the reality of the disease which was slowly wasting him away; no doctor, no prayers, not all the money in the world could save him. His illness was progressing inexorably…

So gradually his awareness of it also grew: 'Yes, I am dying. I will die soon.' When contemplating his own disappearance, his own *fading into nothingness*, it was as if a knife was piercing into his stomach.

In varying orders he went through fear, anxiety, terror, giddiness, denial, contempt, grief, derision, horror, helplessness, rage and resignation. The thought of not being, at the same time made him feel wounded, oppressed, disgusted and thrown into utter despair.

Then, he sank into a deep depression.

He was overwhelmed by the pain of having to leave those he loved, those who needed him… the idea of everything coming to an end shattered him. He had to face and accept his life's failures which were now irreparable; it was too late to try again! The remorse, the shame… words of love and friendship he had never managed to utter, projects never to be completed. He remembered all the things he had put off till tomorrow throughout his entire life. Yet he still wanted to try and resist… But nothing could help him evade this other thought: 'No one has the least importance for the future of this world. Life itself never stops, but mine will end.' Gradually, he came to terms with the idea of losing himself and the world; he learned to tame his panic about not existing, and the overwhelming silence of death that would destroy him. 'I am confusing fear of death and death', he thought. 'There is no will and no desire without a body, no fear without a body, no me without a body. There is no ego in death. Without a body, without a 'me' who should be afraid of death? What is there to be afraid of? I don't have to dread anything about death! Death is the end of dreading. But can I accept death...? No. Am I ready to die now...? No. Not yet.'

He put his affairs in order, called his friends together and told them: 'Don't be sad when I'm dead, because I won't be. I am happy with my life. I did what I could. I have seen misery and beauty. I have travelled the world. I have loved and was loved. I have sometimes won and sometimes lost. Tomorrow will be a new day, and the next night will be as beautiful as a night can be. Nothing will stop. Nothing should stop.'

His ties to the world were gradually severed and he managed to regard death as a new adventure, in just the same way that life had been.

*'Birth, not life, is opposed to death. Before our birth, could we imagine life? Why try to imagine what follows death? Death gives fright to the imagination because it is precisely that which cannot be imagined,' Aryadeva.*

# Dying

*In his essay "Western attitudes toward death in the Middle Ages", Philippe Aries describes the traditional outlook towards death which prevailed for centuries. He called it "the tamed death" as opposed to death nowadays being seen as "wild" due to the fact that it is hidden, denied, suppressed, and helplessly feared.*

'In days of old, dying was a public ceremony presided over by the dying person. It was not overly dramatic and the process was played out in several stages.

The first one was to openly regret life in a sad but restrained recollection of loved ones and belongings. This emotion doesn't last. It is a stage of the ritual. Following the lament for passing of life is the sharing out of possessions, and then forgiveness of brothers in arms and the attending friends and family, who were always numerous, surrounding the bed of the dying: "I forgive you here and before God." Then the dying recommends his survivors to God.

It's time to forget the world and think about God. The dying one does this by beating his breast, expressing regret for his sins, and then turning to the Creator, he says: "True Father, save my soul from all dangers..."

At this time comes the only ecclesiastical act, the absolution given by the priest, who reads the Psalms, the *Libera*. He passes incense over the body and sprinkles holy water over him.

After the last prayer, everyone waits for death to come and

there is no reason for it to be long in coming. If it so happens that death takes a long time to come, the dying person waits in silence. He says his last prayer and utters not a single word thereafter.'[91]

[91]. Fragments from Commentaries on the Song of Roland by Philippe Ariès, *Western attitudes toward death in the Middle Ages*, 1975, Edition du Seuil.

## The death of Kalu Rinpoche

Bokar Rinpoche recounts the passing away of the great Tibetan master, Khyabdje Kalu Rinpoche:

'Shortly before his death, his nephew inquired about his health. The master replied:

"Day is the meditation on the experience of illusion. Night is the meditation on the experience of dream."

When his condition suddenly deteriorated, Kalu Rinpoche asked to sit upright. He assumed the meditation posture, his lips moved slowly and his eyes were wide open.

A deep sense of peace and happiness settled in between us all and spread through our minds. Everyone present felt that the indescribable happiness filling us was merely a pale glimmer of what was alighting Rinpoche's mind.

Slowly Rinpoche's gaze and eyelids drooped and his breathing ceased. This was the passing into deep meditation.

The doctor and the nurse wanted to use special means to restore his breathing, but Chatral Rinpoche asked for Rinpoche to be left in peace.'[92]

[92]. Revue Dharma, Hommage to Khyabdje Kalou Rinpoche: 1904-1989, Number 6.

## Heaven

Rabbi Moshe Teitelbaum used to write his dreams down. This one was found in his notebooks:

'I went to the heaven of the *Tannaim*, the great doctors of the law. There, I saw one doctor seated, wearing a fur cap, meditating on the treaty of the First Door. There was nothing else. This greatly astonished me:

"Impossible, this can't be heaven!" I exclaimed.

But the angels told me:

"You think that the *Tannaim* are in heaven? It's not so. It's heaven which is found in the *Tannaim*."'[93]

*"The* Chekhina, *the Divine Presence, dwells over the head of those who study the Torah (Bible), it is said, because studying the Torah and rejoicing in it is equivalent to practicing all the commandments at once. So, Heaven, the reward of the saintly, is unlikely to be a place they go to after death, but a way in which they perceive, live and act in the world.*

---

[93]. Jerome Mintz, *Legends of the Hassidim* ; University of Chicago Press, 1974. Harry Rabinovicz, *Hassidism : The Movement and its Masters ; Jason Aronson Inc. ;* 1988.

## The Three Messengers

One day, Yama, the Lord of death, questioned a man who was brought before him.

'Have you not met my three messengers?'

'No, I never saw any messengers.'

'Have you never met the old man, bent with age, walking with a cane?'

'Oh yes Lord, I often came across such people,' the man answered.

'Well, if you're here now, it's because you have not recognized in the old man the messenger of the truth of decay. Have you not seen the poor man, alone and ill?'

'Lord, I've seen many.'

'Well, you're here now because you didn't see in that man the messenger of the truth of suffering. Haven't you seen the dead man?'

'I saw many dead people, my Lord.'

'Well, you're here now because you haven't understood the dead man to be the messenger of the truth of impermanence. If you had recognized my three messengers, you wouldn't be seeing me, you would be free from wanting a life with all of its suffering, you wouldn't still be returning to the cycle of deaths and births, and feeling surprised to be in it. Most men say: Death is but an illusion. Those contemplating the certainty of death are on the path to serenity.'[94]

---

94. From *The teaching of Buddha*, Bukkyo Dendo Kyokai, Tokyo, Japan, 1979.

## After me

*Where the movement? Where the rest?*
*Towards which shore will you cross, Ô my heart?*
*There is no road on that shore,*
*Neither a raft nor any ferryman,*
*Neither earth nor heavens, nor time.*
*You will find nothing in this emptiness.*

*Kabir*

In the evening at the yeshiva, Rabbi Naphtali studied and commented on the Bible with a few disciples. One of them was obsessed with a particular verse from the Scriptures: "Before me no God was formed and there will be none after me." (Isaiah 43:10) This disciple often returned to the same question:

'How can there be a *before* and an *after* for God who has no beginning or end?'

One day, the Rabbi decided to give him an answer:

'God is a creator. Without a Creation and without a creature, there is no creator. If God ever stops creating, he ceases to be. "Before me no God was ever formed," the prophet Isaiah said. This means that God only exists with you. It would be in vain to try to conceive of the existence of God if there were no humans.

"And there will be none after me," means: an *after me* does not exist. It would also be in vain to tell impossible stories and make false promises about an after *me* that does not exist.'[95]

*The ultimate maze is life itself. When one finds death, is this finally an exit?*

[95]. On an idea of Rabbi Naphtali liberally adapted from a Hassidic tale. The quote is Isaiah 43:10. A yeshiva is an institute of learning where students study sacred texts.

# Till you return to the earth...

*The Midrash quotes this comment: In the Bible of Rabbi Meir, you find at the end of the sixth day: "God saw everything he had done..." and instead of "And here, it was very good (tov mé'od)", it is written: "And here, death was good (tov mot'). According to Rabbi Meir, the extreme good bears a very close resemblance to death.*[96]

Rabbi Isaac Goldman was commenting on the verse
'God told the Adam (mankind): *By the sweat of your brow, you will eat bread, till you return to the earth from which you were taken, for you are dust and to dust you shall return.*
"'Death," says Maimonides, who was a doctor, "is the end of form." "Tradition teaches," the Midrash quotes: *Everything originating in birth dies and rots, is created and does not create. What does not originate in birth does not die or rot, creates and is not created. The Adams were created; they must die.'* No human has ever been immortal. What God creates is not immutable.
So, *By the sweat of your brow, you will eat bread*, God said to the Adam, and then, in a demonstration of love that reveals the infinite mercy of God, he reassured him: *till you return to the earth from which you were taken.*
Till... If you associate death with evil or punishment, as if it were obvious or if you think we should be afraid of dying, or if you confuse your fear of death with death itself, or if, with

[96]. Commentaries on Geneses 1:31 : Midrash Rabba; Geneses Rabba IX: 5;

some painful anticipated nostalgia, you wish your own reality to be infinite and immortal, if you come to believe that life would be wonderful if it was endless… then this verse will come across as the sentence of a merciless judge.

But from the emotionless point of view of God, for whom all is always well, from the point of view of a man who, just like the fellow students of Rabbi Simeon, can say of something he has experienced, "if I had come to this world for this alone it would have sufficed," from the point of view of wisdom that nothing moves for long, from the point of view of a pious man who knows and longs for God, we can understand this as a limit, a measure: *only until…* We are not obliged to take death to be an evil.

God does not condemn the Adam to death; he just reminds him that he is dust. Existence contains within itself the condition of its own end, the ultimate exit from time and suffering. *By the sweat of your brow, you will eat bread…* but only *until you return to the earth*. It is like saying: "don't worry, life is not eternal". This reserve, this moderation, this measure, is mercy. God offers man the certainty of death as the most authentic proof of his benevolence.

Each part of thc infinitc is infinitc. The infinite is infinitely infinite. But each part of the infinite is not eternal. Eternity is infinitely the same - extremely unexciting. Thank God, life is not eternal. Nothing is eternal. The infinite is the eternally different and it includes death.

*Forever* is not the exact opposite of *never*: they don't weigh the same. *Forever* matters more, is much more serious than *never*. Better *never* than *ever*. If you were never born, you

would not regret it, but if you were forever alive, it might become tedious with time... However if it's not forever, you can accept to live for a while...
The kiss by which God takes back a man's breath is a kiss of love just like the kiss by which he gave it."[97]

*'Life is full of misery, loneliness, and suffering and it's all over much too soon!' Woody Allen.*

[97]. *By the sweat of your brow...* Genesis 3: 19 and Ecclesiast 12:7.

## Rebirth

*The Hindu and Buddhist traditions include a belief in the rebirth of the self. In the twentieth century, this belief has spread into the Christian world through the teachings of Tibetan lamas and Hindu gurus coming to the West.*

*The Christian perspective of death is characterised by its negation. It asserts that death does not exist since the soul finds salvation in life after death - the real eternal life - in resurrection to another world: a desirable heaven, or an unimaginable hell of suffering or non-existence. The soul is personal and so too is salvation.*

*Westerners who have a Christian background are individualists who believe in their permanence; they have received the rebirth hypothesis as a new form of salvation, and they often take it as a new way to deny death. They call it reincarnation, instead of rebirth. 'I shall not really die, I'm just going to change body!' they think and are pacified by this. They contemplate their coming back to life as a consolation for having to die.*

*A Hindu or a Buddhist doesn't hope to sur-vive death, they try not to under-die life. They wish to escape the cycle of births and really die.*

*This doctrine is taught in different ways, each aimed at a larger level of awareness. Here, in a guru - disciple dialogue, are three ways of considering the issue.*

'Lama, sentient beings are born and die. Is it true that we come back to life after we die?'

'What do you think?'
'I don't know. If sentient beings disappear completely, what was the purpose of their life? And if they are reborn after death, do they ever really die? Do they ever find rest? Will we go to a paradise, in another world, will we return to this world or will we just become nothing?'
'Why are you concerned about what happens after life? Are you free of all worldly ties?'
'No, Lama,' the disciple replied humbly.
'Then see in your attachments what is binding you to yourself. And strive to free yourself from them.'
'But what about death?' the disciple insisted.
'If we die still attached to life, we will return in life. If we reach liberation during life time, we will be freed from the cycle of rebirth. We reap as we sow.'
A few months passed. One day the disciple asked the same question again. His beloved Lama replied:
'Life consists of three characteristics, *anitya* impermanence, *dukkha*, suffering and *anatma*, no-self, no soul, no intrinsic and eternal identity.
Everything is made of different components. We call a cart the assembly of a wooden platform with wheels, shafts, nails, etc. And each of these parts is itself made, shaped or formed from something else. Therefore the name we give something is a convention, but the reality of that thing is dependent, conditional, impermanent, related to circumstances, and exists only in the domain of names and forms. The same is also true for living beings. An Individual or self is the name we give to the gathered forces and elements that constitute a living being.

So how could something that exists only due to the forces and elements that make it up continue existing after the dispersion of these forces and elements?'

'Is there not a mind or a soul, or something that survives death?'

'Since there is no self, how can you imagine a mind or a soul of the self?'

'Yet, we conceive the idea of a self and we grasp on to it.'

'Yes and we can also free ourselves from it. "What appears in the mind and disappears in the mind is nothing but the mind itself," Patanjali taught. Give up any hope of a result.

*Anatma* means that there is no self, no self identity and no eternal self, and therefore no transmigration of a "self", or any future liberation of a "self". You can only get liberation in the moment, a moment at a time. Stop even desiring liberation, because that's what is preventing you from finding it.'

The disciple realized that his Lama did not always answer the same way to the same question. He asked his master again a few months later. This time, his Lama replied:

'A life is created. It produces the belief in the existence of a self. We can break free of this self simply by ceasing to cling to this belief.'

'But what happens after death?' the disciple persisted.

'Each life can be compared to a drop of consciousness' the Lama said. 'At the time of death that drop goes back to the ocean of the impersonal consciousness (Alayavijnana) and dissolves in it. Therefore it brings to it the experience of its life. Later, when a drop from this ocean becomes a new life, is it the same drop or another one?'

'It's the same… and it's is not the same…'

'Why is that?'
'Because it was mixed with the others.'
'Exactly. It is the same and yet not the same, because the new drop is made up of something from all the others. There is no direct passage from one life to another, no individual rebirth. The drop and the ocean is an image to help us understand that life is born in a context that all previous lives have prepared.'
'But you said that we reap what we sow.'
'All sentient beings are born from this ocean from which we arise as well. The same will be in all the other lives as well. Thus we will reap what we have sown, and what has been sown by all the others as well.'

*Jesus was a Jew, just as Buddha was a Hindu. They both had roots in pre-existing religions, and they both have become the founding figure of a new one. Jesus introduced life after death into Judaism which spoke of none. Buddha subtracted a personal soul, an* atma *or a* self, *from the Hindu religion of his birth. However many schools of Buddhism reintroduced it.*
*The Dalai Lama explains: 'The idea of reincarnation is integrated into the philosophical framework of Buddhism. It's a kinetic energy (motive force) which is a result of the previous life. It isn't a teaching of the Buddha. The Buddha's contribution is to show that there is no soul or self which transmigrates.*
*But a person having reached a high degree of spiritual evolution is assumed to be able to direct, at the time of his death, this flow of energy in a particular direction, giving birth to a* tulku *(an emanation of a particular lama)'*

## Which Death?

*A Muslim told a Sufi:*
*'We are indeed similar. We both read the Koran, and we both believe in the Prophet...*
*'No, we're not the same,' the Sufi interrupted, 'we are different. You hope for Heaven, while I seek God.*

'The old masters used to tell the following story,' said Sheikh Assam:
"A man on his deathbed was going through the maze of his thoughts, desires and preconceptions. From time to time, he remembered and prayed to Allah for mercy; he wished that his soul was eternal; he yearned for a paradise which he tried to imagine. But he also feared hell, and regretted many evil deeds.
Finally death took him. He breathed his last breath. Now dead, he discovered in amazement that he still existed, but just as he was before. His thoughts, desires and preconceptions recreated exactly the same world he had left, as if he was not gone. Throughout his life he had been afraid of death, and now dead he was still afraid, but this time he knew he should be afraid of himself."
The effect of thoughts or hopes or fears is to create or perpetuate their author,' Sheikh Assam further explained. 'You never think without yourself, you never want anything without yourself. So the question death is posing is: shall I die with my me or without my me?
Death is exactly what you want it to be. Because while you

are alive, death is no different than what you think of it. And then after death, you might become what you want and what you fear.

If there isn't a me outlasting life, you won't be aware of it. But if there is one, you have to fear your me… when it fails to die.

To die means to stop desiring and imagining, to stop creating yourself. He who hopes for God in paradise, doesn't really love God; he doesn't truly want paradise. First and foremost he imagines himself in the circumstances he imagines. His ego is so big that there is nothing else he wants as much as his "me". How could he really reach Heaven? How would he recognize God, which is the unimaginable?

The problem is wanting. Death calls us to nothingness.

The Sufi endeavours to die before death and thus to know the immortality of the uncreated. He makes sure that, after death, there is no more death."[98]

---

[98]. Cheikh Assam, in Patrick Levy, *Dieu croit-il en Dieu ?*, Question de/Albin Michel; 1993.

## That which nothing can reach

Fixed in silence
He reaches perfect emptiness.
Maintaining total inner peace
He contemplates the appearance of things.
However plentiful beings and things may be,
He contemplates their appearance and their disappearance.
Each thing grows and flourishes before returning to its source.
Returning to the source is called silence
Silence is to find the order of things
The order enables one to find permanence.
Permanence enables one to find awakening
Not being awakened leads to confusion
Knowing awakening, the mind is impartial
Impartiality is unprejudiced
The unprejudiced one is universal
The universal one is at one with the Tao (the Way).
At one with the Tao, merging into the Way,
Nothing can be harmful
Not even death.[99]

[99]. Lao Tzu, *Tao Te Ching*, XVI.

# IX

## Hapiness and Sorrow

*Happiness and unhappiness are extremely relative. Everyone knows that if something is pleasant for one person it won't always be the same for another. It all depends, as they say. Something that delights me today may bore me to death tomorrow.*

*'Everything in the universe is impermanent,' taught Khenpo Tsultrim. Impermanence is the only reality. No strength, no power, no will has ever managed to stop change. Everything changes, a friend turns out to be an enemy, life later becomes death, and this develops into that. How then, do we overcome impermanence?*

*Love your enemy as you would love your friend, so if your friend becomes an enemy, nothing will have changed for you. Have the same attitude toward all events: the happy and the unhappy ones, life and death, this or that. Only equanimity can transcend change. It's the only way to overcome impermanence and death.'*

*Equanimity is a little known virtue. It is sometimes taken to mean that all things are equal. However things are indeed different. At times certain things are subjectively or objectively preferable to others. Yet whilst it is true that things are unequal, everything can be considered from a distance, which is neither resignation nor indifference, but the wisdom of detachment.*

*Pleasure is not pain, life is not death but from a certain perspective both can be seen merely as events. Moreover happiness inevitably ceases and in the same way troubles also come to an end.*

*Someone who knows this will not always be renowned for their erudition. Sometimes a wise man looks quite ordinary.*

## Who is rich?

One day, at King Solomon's court, an old man asked this question to the monarch renowned for his wisdom:
'What is a rich man?'
From the top of his golden throne encrusted with rubies King Solomon asked the assembly to give an answer. A shop keeper said:
'A rich man has a hundred ingots of gold, or more.'
'How many do you own?' the King asked.
'Fifty, my lord.'
A farmer spoke:
'A rich man has a large herd.'
'Is yours large enough?'
'I have but a thousand cattle, O king.'
A priest said:
'A rich man is blessed with many sons: ten healthy ones at least!'
'How many sons do you have?'
'Only five, my Lord.'
'Behold,' King Solomon concluded, addressing the old man, 'everyone knows what a rich man is, but nobody is rich. There is no rich man.'
A poor man answered timidly:
'The man who, looking at what he has, sees what he wants, is a rich man.'
'The world is as we see it,' added King Solomon complementing the poor man's wisdom. 'If we lay down conditions for our happiness, it becomes inaccessible or short lived. Happiness is the result of renunciation and is not the fruit of success. Wisdom is the only wealth which brings happiness. It is something we can never own; however everyone can be inspired by it.'

## The Book of Grievances

One day the inhabitants of the earth gathered together to send God a book of grievances.

The spiders complained that stags, walking through the forest, tore away their webs. The stags were afraid of the lions which ate them. The lions thought stags could run much too fast and were too difficult to catch.

Mosquitoes lamented about the wind blowing them away from their targets, and the wind accused the mountains of creating obstacles for its journey. The mountains said that rain eroded them, and the rain complained about the wind.

Mice were scared of the owls, which ate them, and owls demanded longer nights, for hunting.

The hens accused foxes of crimes against the henhouse, and foxes denounced humans for genocide against their race. As for humans, they could never agree amongst themselves.

The southerners wanted the sun to be less hot, northerners wanted it to be warmer. Others wanted rain. Tribes and countries at war were calling out to God for help.

Many complained about their neighbours; this one had built a house overshadowing that one's garden; an old shop keeper protested that a new store was unfair competition for him; the inhabitants of this village did not practice the right religion, and they ate nettles!

The poor argued that the rich were happier, they felt it wasn't fair; the wealthy claimed that fairness was not the issue and demanded that there be much fewer beggars. Landowners said labour was too expensive. Workers said wages were too low. The kings demanded more discipline. Thieves cursed the doors and locks. Farmers cried out that the earth was too low!

God received this petition in which everyone living on Earth was complaining about something. To satisfy everyone he would have get rid of everyone else. And that would leave no one!

'They are so skilful in describing the difficulties of their situations, but in terms of the wisdom which acknowledges their benefits they are severely lacking,' So God told those who could hear him. 'I understand you all, but you don't understand me or anybody else. You are unable to appreciate the nature of the world. I am the sun and the shade, I am the cold and the heat, the rain and drought, I am the hen and the fox, I am the friend and the enemy. I am this one's bliss and that one's sorrow, I am the one who eats and also the one who is eaten. This world is but a single being. Individuality is an illusion.'

# The Poor Peasant and his White Horse

*When we are overwhelmed by an adversity, how can we be sure that in the end it will not turn out to be a blessing? Haven't we all experienced that?*
*How can we know if the success we greet with open arms will not eventually turn into a disaster? Taking circumstances as they come with equanimity and without having an opinion is much better.*

A poor old peasant had one single possession: a beautiful white horse which even made the king himself envious. The king wanted to buy it from him, however the old man always refused to sell it. One day his white horse disappeared. The neighbours of the old man gathered together and criticized him:
'What a fool you are! You could have sold your horse and freed yourself from poverty, and now it has been stolen… This is really bad luck.'
'All we can say,' the old man replied, 'is that my horse is gone. We don't know if it was stolen and we don't know if it's misfortune.'
Sometime later, the white horse returned to the paddock followed by a dozen wild horses.
This time his neighbours congratulated the old man:
'You were right. What happened to you was great luck. You are rich now.'
'All we can say,' the old man replied, 'is that my horse is back. We don't know if it is lucky or unlucky.'

The old man's only son set to work in order to break the horses in. But doing this he fell down and broke both his legs. The old man's neighbours gathered once again:
'Well after all, it seems it was trouble rather than good luck! Now that your son is injured, who will support your family?'
'You are all obsessed about having an opinion on everything,' the old man replied. 'All we know is that my son broke his legs. We don't know if it is good or bad luck.'
A few weeks later, the kingdom went to war. All the young men were conscripts, except the son of the old man who could not walk. Most young people would never return from the battle fields. The old man's neighbours met again:
'You were right, it wasn't bad luck but good fortune that your son broke his legs.'
'Again, no one knows that,' the old man replied patiently.[100]

[100]. Chinese Wisdom adapted from Lie tzu, Foreign Languages Press, Beijing.

## What Hardship?

A devotee was puzzled by a question. He went to his Rabbi to ask him about it:

'It is said that we should rejoice in the same way for the good and the bad, for happiness and sorrow that God grants us. Thanking for the good, that's easy to understand, but being grateful for hardships and pain, what does that mean? How is this possible?'

The rabbi thought about his for a moment, then said:

'I can't help you. You better go and ask this question to Rabbi Zusia of Anipoli.'

One day, our man decided to go to Anipoli. In that village, he could find no house belonging to a rabbi. He asked someone for directions. He was pointed out, further away, to the edge of the forest where there was an old house. So he headed off in that direction.

He had to walk almost a mile along a muddy road before he got there. It was a rickety old house. The walls were held up by props, and the roof had holes in several places and almost all the windows were broken. The winter was harsh yet there was no smoke coming out of the chimney. In addition to this he heard the loud and crude voice of the lady of the house. A shrew!

'Here I am in the lair of sorrow,' he thought. At that time, Rabbi Zusia came out, saw the man and invited him in for a cup of tea. The house was even more dilapidated inside and the tea was little more than faintly coloured water. The man did not receive even the slightest smile from the hostess.

Nevertheless the devotee had come to ask a question and so he asked it:
'It is taught that we should bless God and thank him for both happiness and sorrow. For happiness, I understand, but for sorrow and pain, how is this possible?'
'What sorrow? Which pain? I don't know any,' the Rabbi answered. 'I don't need anything, and I don't miss anything. I have never known suffering and misfortune.'

*A few years ago I was staying in a monastery. When the bell rang to announce lunch or dinner time, everybody started walking to the refectory. As I was heading to the refectory, I naturally looked towards it, in that direction. But I was struck by the behaviour of the monks: as they were walking to the refectory, they were looking down at their feet.*
*In order to avoid the temptation of wanting to get there before having walked the whole way in full awareness, the monks avoided looking at their destination. They leaned over and watched their steps.*
*Patience can be found in gazing into the horizon which unfurls at our feet. Serenity, peace and joy can also be found right there.*

## A Good Investment

A man was saving part of his income every day. After a few years, he had accumulated a substantial amount of money. But with the growth of his savings his worries had also grown. He was constantly afraid of thieves.

He decided to build a beautiful house, so he would no longer have to look after the money day and night. But when the house was built, he began to dread fire. He even lost sleep over it!

He sold his house and deposited the money in a savings account, in a bank. 'But banks can be robbed, or go bankrupt,' he now feared. So he withdrew his money from the bank. The next day it burnt down, but our man was not worried as his money was now at home, in a safe.

However fear came back to haunt him. He started worrying about his children poisoning him and then opening his safe.

One day, a charitable organization asked him for a contribution to build an orphanage. The man gave all his savings.

From then on, he was no longer afraid of anything and lived in peace. He had the reputation of a noble and generous man and the orphanage was named after him.

It still exists; and a few decades since, many children still pay tribute to this man's name every day.

*Ten powerful things were created: the rock is hard, but it can be cut by iron; the iron is hard, but it can be melted by fire; fire is powerful but water can extinguish it; the water is powerful but clouds retain it; clouds are strong but the wind scatters them; the wind is strong but the body resists it; the body is tough but fear can break it; fear is great, but wine subdues it; wine is powerful but sleep dispels drunkenness; Death is the most powerful of all these things, yet charity delivers us from death.*[101]

101. Talmud of Babylon, Baba Bathra 10b. The last sentence: Proverbs 10:2.

# The Broken Bowl

*A man understands the meaning of happiness the day he starts enjoying everything whilst being attached to nothing, said Aryadeva.*

Ikyu had been living in a Zen temple with his brother since childhood. One day Ikyu's brother dropped a precious ceremonial tea bowl which the Emperor had offered his master long ago. The bowl was broken. The master would be hurt or perhaps he would fly into a rage upon his return to the temple. Ikyu calmed his brother down:

'Don't worry. I have gained some measure of wisdom. I'll speak to the master.'[102]

He took the pieces of the bowl and put them in the sleeve of his kimono. He then went and stood on the temple's steps. Upon seeing the master, he went to meet him and asked him the following question:

'Master, are men destined to die, or do they not die?'

'They certainly die,' the master replied. 'Even the Buddha died.'

Ikyu nodded, then added:

'And what about objects? Are they permanent or impermanent? Are they destructible or eternal?'

'Anything having form must necessarily disappear. Nothing in this world is eternal. Everything changes, everything dies. Buddha taught this, and observation always confirms it.

Ikyu nodded.

---

102. Zen tale from Japan : *Zen, a way of life*, Seshin Press, 1972, Kyoto.

'So everything is perishable,' he said, feigning grief. 'So we should not weep, or lament over what has gone. And grieving over a loss is like resisting destiny.

'Definitely! What are you trying to say?' the master asked.

Ikyu then took the pieces of the broken bowl out of his kimono sleeve and showed them to his master.

# The Tree of Life

In the Garden of Eden, there were all kinds of trees, all of them bearing good fruits, but there were also two special trees: the Tree of Life and the Tree of Knowledge. In some traditions, it is said that the Tree of Life granted everything one wished for, and the Tree of Knowledge bestowed understanding and discernment.

One day, Adam lied down under a tree… He conceived of something soft and fluffy. As soon as this thought had arisen in his mind, he found a comfortable bed next to him. He stretched out on it.

Then he thought it would be nice if a young woman would come and gently massage his legs. As soon as this thought had taken shape, Eve was sitting beside him, massaging his legs. Adam felt supremely happy. Soon he was hungry and thought of delicious dishes. And at once he discovered several dishes lay out before him. He ate and was satisfied and then relaxed on his bed.

His mind fluttered here and there without taking any particular shape, then stopped on a particular concern: 'What if a terrible snake passed by and bit me' he thought, alarmed. In that very instant a big snake sprang onto him and was about to bite him, but Adam thought fast enough: 'No, don't bite me', and *in extremis* the snake didn't bite him.

Being all-powerful is a very heavy burden to bear. It doesn't even guarantee us happiness. If all our thoughts came true immediately, we would constantly have to remain on the alert.

This would prevent any kind of dream or it would be like an endless nightmare.

Adam moved away from that Tree. He even left the Garden of Eden, for he had understood that life has to be lived using one's own strength. From then on he derived sustenance and meaning from his efforts and from pleasure and pain.[103]

[103]. Liberally adapted from *The Wish Tree*, from India; and from Geneses.

## The Treasure

Rabbi Eisik, the son of Rabbi Yankel, lived in Poland in a small village where he was a poor baker. One night he had a strange dream. An old man told him: 'Go to Prague, and once there, under the bridge which leads to the palace, under the third pillar, dig, and you will unearth a treasure.'

A dream is just a dream, and if we were to do everything our dreams suggest we do… But Eisik had the same dream a second, and then a third time. A dream is just a dream, but having the same dream three times makes it an omen!

So he set off to Prague. He made the whole journey on foot. It was long, full of adventures and challenges. He encountered bandits and saints, trust and fear, hunger and hospitality… He discovered life and humanity.

After several weeks, he finally arrived and he found the bridge he had seen in his dream. However a soldier was there, guarding it day and night. Eisik realised how this whole venture was dangerous, absurd, and useless. How could he dig under a bridge in a city without attracting attention?

As he approached to look at the pillar he came too close and the soldier called out to him:

'What are you doing here? What are you standing here waiting for?'

If Eisik told him about his dream, the guard would find the treasure and keep it… But when the soldier threatened to hit him, he told him what had brought him to Prague.

'You've made this long journey because of an absurd dream?' the soldier derided. 'If we all obeyed our dreams, we'd all be travelling endlessly like idiots! Can you believe it, I also had a dream last night. It told me to go to Poland, to Eisik, the baker, son of Yankel, because under his baker's oven, I would find a treasure.

Eisik said nothing. He left the soldier and set off back to his village.

So did he find treasure under his oven? Or had he not already found one from having undertaken this long journey?

The whole earth is full of treasures! Your treasure, the one waiting for you, can be found in yourself, the sage says. Because it is hidden in your dreams.[104]

[104]. There are many variants of this tale: one from the One Thousand and One Nights, night 351 ; in *Seeker after Truth* by Idries Shah; and in the Hassidic tradition told by Rabbi Nahman of Bratzlav and Rabbi Bounam of Pshiskhe, in Martin Buber's Hassidic Tales; and by E. Wiesel, *Célébration hassidique*, Seuil, 1972, Point sagesse. Jerome Mintz, *Legends of the Hassidim* ; University of ChicagoPress, 1974. Harry Rabinovicz, *Hassidism : The Movement and its Masters ; Jason Aronson Inc. ;* 1988. It was used by Paolo Coelho as the framework for "The Alchemist".

# X

# The Meaning

### *Epilogue*

*"The meaning and purpose of life are not outside of us but in us," Krishnamurti said.*[105] *Indeed, if the meaning and the purpose of our life were outside of us, they would be outside of life. Consequently we would never find them. Life would make no sense and have no purpose for a living being during his life.*
*If the meaning belonged to the future, it would forever be elusive, always lying ahead of us. Such a meaning of life would be of no use to us.*
*If the meaning we are looking for belonged to the known, it would necessarily belong to the past. Therefore either we would be enchained in this meaning, and consequently without freedom, or alternatively this meaning would no longer exist since the known is always past and outdated.*
*Perhaps life has no meaning, but every moment of our lives carries whichever one we give to it.*
*We can only seek and find that which arises in the mo-*

[105]. Krishnamurti, The first and last freedom.

*ment of our questioning. It is in the moment that an answer appears as true, yet it is fleeting.*
*We can never grasp reality; at best we can perceive our relationship with it. Knowing that reality is our relationship with something rather than the thing itself, being crazy and wise enough to accept that life has no definitive meaning and purpose, attempting to know and understand the only person to whom we have access, ourselves, that may be, after all, the ultimate meaning of life. Life gives this meaning to everyone, yet most of us never find it...*

## Life gives Everything to Everyone

*I read "The Book of Sand" by Borges, a few years ago. One of the stories in this collection of short stories had impressed me so much that I used to tell it to my friends. One day I read "The Book of Sand" again, but the story I had been telling for so long was not there, not in the way I had been telling it.*
*Just as there is no book, just readings of it (we all read a different book in the same book), so there can be no universal reading of this book which is life itself... Yet meaning is accessible to everyone...*

The King of K had reached the summit of power. One day, he summoned to him the greatest poet in the kingdom. He told him:
'I want you to compose an ode to my fame. Take your time. I'll give you a whole year to do it. And you know how generously I reward my faithful servants.'
The poet went back home and worked tirelessly. He composed an ode in accordance with the most accurate tenets of his time. It combined alliterations and scansions and had an abundance of rhetorical figures. By the end of the year, he had written a long and magnificent eulogy.
Before the assembled court, the poet presented his ode to the king. He read it slowly and with gravity. The king approved of his words nodding his head. At the end, he said to the poet:
'Your work deserves my acclaim. If every kind of literature were to disappear suddenly, we could reconstruct it without

losing anything using your ode. All of it is edifying, yet something is missing. Nobody went pale. Our heart isn't beating any faster. Nobody felt like shouting their war cry. Go home. I'll give you another year to compose an unforgettable ode to my fame. But for now, receive this ring as a token of my appreciation.

The poet spent the whole year rewriting his poem. He endlessly recomposed his ode to his king's fame; he wrote thousands of pages and threw away almost as many. The year ended and he was back in front of the assembled court. He read his ode aloud, which was much shorter than the first one. Then the king said:

'This poem goes beyond and nullifies anything that ever preceded it. It surprises, it astounds, it dazzles. Accept the greatest jewel of the kingdom as a token of my appreciation. However, we can expect the pen that has produced such a remarkable piece of work to produce an even more sublime one.

Another year passed. This time the poet couldn't write anything. When the day came to appear before the king's court, he had no manuscript to offer.

'Have you not written an ode?' the king inquired.

'I have, Majesty,' the poet said. 'But I dare not say it. It is only one word long. I can utter it only to you.'

The poet asked the king to grant him a moment of conversation.

'Come closer,' the king said.

That day, a merchant who had travelled to the ends of the world had shown his most precious goods to the monarch. He was still there, quite close when the poet said the single word of his ode in the ear of the king who, having heard it, was filled with wonder. On this occasion, he did turn pale and his heart did beat faster. When he regained his composure, he realized that the merchant might also have heard the single word of the ode. In doubt, the king sentenced him to death the very next day. Meanwhile, he was thrown into prison for the night.

Before dawn, a terrible storm swept over the city. Lightning struck the wall of the prison which fell down and collapsed. The merchant took his chance and escaped.

He then began an endless peregrination which was to become his life. He fled without ever stopping. He became a thief, a public writer, a blacksmith, a lumberjack, a rower, a usurer, an arms dealer, a slave trader, and in turn was enslaved himself and escaped. He loved, was loved, fought a duel, came to work as a stonemason, then as a mercenary… was a vagrant then a vagabond again.

What was the one word he had not heard? Along his endless flight a missionary suggested "God", but he doubted that an all powerful, benevolent one watched over him. A woman thought it might be "Love", he succumbed to her charms, but left her before dawn on a listless morning. A child showed him "Innocence", he didn't consider himself guilty or impure. A hermit proposed "Renunciation", he renounced it immediately. An old man moaned "Decrepitude", a dying man cried "Death", a funeral pir suggested Ashes a wise man sighed "Vanity". None of these words alone resonated like the most sublime hymn. None of them could have brought him a death sentence. Not one of them could have made the king turn pale and his heart beat faster.

One evening, along one of the world's many roads, he knocked on the door of a house, requesting hospitality. Inside, an old man was dying.

'Do you recognize me?' the old man asked.

'Yes, I do recognize you. You are the poet from the kingdom of K.'

His face looked so old that the merchant could not help thinking that he had also become a very old man.

'Did you hear the word?' the poet asked faintly.

'No. The moment you spoke a noise prevented me from hearing.'

'But you understood…'

'Yes, now I understand. You said *Ramka*, which, means "wonder" and in your tongue it means "Life gives everything to everyone, but most men are unaware of it."'[106]

[106]. From an idea of Luis Borgès, *The Book of Sand*.

# Acknowledgments

I would like to thank Odile Poisson who gave me the idea of undertaking this project; and Nourit Masson-Sekine for her help since its very beginning.

I also wish to express my deep appreciation to my editor, Ms Aditi Maheshwari from Vani Prakashan, for her enthusiasm concerning this project, and to my translator, Andy Paice, for his dedicated and precise work.

